T0277100

THE
EMPLOYEE
EXPERIENCE
REVOLUTION

THE
EMPLOYEE
EXPERIENCE
REVOLUTION

*Increase Morale, Retain Your Workforce,
and Drive Business Growth*

JOHN R. DiJULIUS III
& DAVID D. MURRAY

GREENLEAF
BOOK GROUP PRESS

Published by Greenleaf Book Group Press
Austin, Texas
www.gbgpress.com

Distributed by Greenleaf Book Group

For ordering information or special discounts for bulk purchases, please contact Greenleaf Book Group at PO Box 91869, Austin, TX 78709, 512.891.6100.

Design and composition by Greenleaf Book Group and Kim Lance
Cover design by Greenleaf Book Group and Kim Lance

Publisher's Cataloging-in-Publication data is available.

Print ISBN: 979-8-88645-192-4

eBook ISBN 979-8-88645-193-1

To offset the number of trees consumed in the printing of our books, Greenleaf donates a portion of the proceeds from each printing to the Arbor Day Foundation. Greenleaf Book Group has replaced over 50,000 trees since 2007.

Printed in the United States of America on acid-free paper

24 25 26 27 28 29 30 31   10 9 8 7 6 5 4 3 2 1

First Edition

CONTENTS

INTRODUCTION
WHY THIS BOOK? WHY NOW?

The term "accidental manager" is not new. The concept has been around for a while. A quick definition of an accidental manager is a manager who is "all title and no training." While accidental managers have been around for a while, there has been a sharp spike since the pandemic. In a 2019 study conducted by The Chartered Management Institute, 68 percent of the managers studied were considered accidental—in management positions without adequate training. In a similar study conducted in October of 2023, that number shot up to 82 percent—with 25 percent of those being in senior leadership positions.[1]

The effects of accidental managers can be drastic. Untrained managers contribute to higher turnover in organizations and can damage company cultures. In addition, employees reporting to accidental managers are much more likely to feel less satisfied with their jobs, less valued, and less motivated.

As this trend continues to move in the wrong direction, the research also tells us once bad management has taken root within an organization, it is very difficult to right the ship. *The Employee Experience Revolution* was written to do just that—help right the ship. Authors John DiJulius and Dave Murray have a combined

70 years of experience working in, working with, and leading organizations that create great cultures and employee experience. Here is a brief overview as to why employee experience is important to John and Dave . . .

Why employee experience is important to me

It is often said that our jobs don't define us, but our jobs and careers are a huge part of who we are. Work is a significant amount of the time we spend alive. Every leader should realize that work needs to be rewarding in addition to the financial compensation one receives. As leaders we need to build the type of company that helps employees be proud of the work they do, allow them to become their best selves, and have an opportunity to live their best lives.

—John DiJulius

Why employee experience is important to me

Internal culture and employee experience have always been very important to me, primarily because I have worked in some cultures that could have used a little bit of help. Before joining The DiJulius Group in 2013, I had spent most of my career in the sports and entertainment industry. I truly loved each and every role I had, as well as each organization I had the good fortune to be a part of, but one thing always stood out to me. We would lose a lot of really good people on a regular basis, and I eventually realized that the culture was not all that great. Here is an example. I specifically remember the scene. Sales were down, we were reaching a point where we might miss an important sales goal. The leader of the department called everyone on the sales team into the open area of the office and shared this. He said as a team and as individuals, none of us were performing up to expectations, and then he shared what to me were the magic words for the problem. He said, "There are 100 other people out there right now that would kill for your job . . . and not only that . . . they'd take it for less money."

I am not sure what the desired outcome of that meeting was. Perhaps the thought process was that this group of young sales representatives would burst through the door to get to their phones, make sales, and save the day by hitting the goal number. But I can tell you how it made me feel. In an instant—the amount of time it took to say two sentences—I no longer felt as if I was in the right place. I no longer felt that I was with an organization concerned about my growth as an ongoing member of the team. That was probably not the intent of the speech. The speech was most likely delivered to motivate sales and hit a number. But I can tell you many people felt unmotivated after it took place. Because of that, helping companies create a strong culture has become a focus of mine.

Now, let's get you started on your Employee Experience Revolution.

—Dave Murray

ACKNOWLEDGMENTS

We would like to thank our DiJulius Group teammates, both past and present, for helping us create this book. From conducting research, to working with our client base producing incredible results, every member of our team has lent a hand in this books' production. Thank you to Denise Thompson, Claudia Medica, Lindsey Friedel, Nicole Paul, Cal DiJulius, and Jessica Bound-Pischel!

Thank you to my incredible family Claudia, Johnni, Cal, & Bo. Nothing is more important to me than your love. I am the luckiest person in the world.

—John

I first need to thank my co-author and mentor, John DiJulius. John, your dedication to our purpose of creating a Customer Service Revolution is inspiring to see, and I am thankful that you brought me along on this employee experience journey. It has been an honor!

I am excited to have the opportunity to thank my amazing family for their unwavering support throughout my entire career. Whether it was the 14-hour days back in my pro sports days, or my spending extra time researching and writing this book, my family has always been there for me. A special shout-out to my wonderful wife, Tracy, and my three amazing kids—Ella, Lilly, and Will!

I also need to thank my amazing mom, Ellen, for all of her hard work and support from my early years to today. She has been there for me each and every day.

And finally, I need to thank my Dad, Jerry. While we were not always together physically, he was always just a phone call away with any support I needed. While it is sad that he is not still with us to see this day, this book was written in his memory. I know he would have been so proud, and we miss him every day.

—Dave

1

WE ARE IN A RECESSION . . .
A CUSTOMER EXPERIENCE RECESSION

"A great customer experience is always powered by a great employee experience."

—JOHN DiJULIUS III

B usiness leaders and economists are always obsessing over a recession. Is it coming, has it started, how long will it last? One of our favorite quotes around this topic is, "Economists have accurately predicted nine of the last five recessions." Which basically means, no expert knows what the hell they are talking about when they try to predict what the economy will or won't do. However, one thing is certain: We are in one of the worst customer service recessions ever, and since 2018, this recession has been dropping faster than the Titanic.

The American Customer Satisfaction Index (ACSI), a national customer satisfaction report measuring nearly every industry, reported that overall customer satisfaction has been spiraling out of control since '18, hitting its lowest score in decades in '22! (See Image 1.1.)

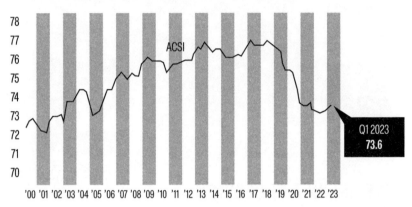

The American Customer Satisfaction Index (ACSI) 2000–2023

ACSI

Q1 2023
73.6

'00 '01 '02 '03 '04 '05 '06 '07 '08 '09 '10 '11 '12 '13 '14 '15 '16 '17 '18 '19 '20 '21 '22 '23

© 2023 American Customer Satisfaction Index. All Rights Reserved.

Image 1.1

There are several reasons for the rapid descent in overall customer satisfaction. Although the COVID-19 pandemic certainly played a role, the fall in customer satisfaction began several years before. Between 2010 and 2022, the US had one of the strongest economic stretches in its history. A booming economy can lead some businesses to rapid growth and, as a consequence, less focus on their customers' and employees' experience. This leads to one of our favorite quotes: "Even a turkey can fly in a tornado."

However, the economic boom is only one of the reasons for the customer service recession. From 2010 to 2019, about 70 percent of companies had declining or flat customer satisfaction scores. Since then, American customers have become even more dissatisfied.[1]

What does customer experience have to do with the employee experience?

A company's customer satisfaction scores are merely a lagging indicator of several symptoms. Due to an unprecedented booming economy, leaders start taking shortcuts, focusing solely on sales and profit, reducing their hiring standards to fill positions, expecting and demanding more of their employees. Investing in the employee culture and customer experience becomes a low priority. All of this causes employee burnout, low employee morale, high turnover, inconsistent experiences, and customer frustration.

The pandemic didn't change what was happening in customer and employee experience; it accelerated the trends. The COVID-19 pandemic lit the match. As a result, the Great Resignation was born—a mass, voluntary exodus from the workforce. Turnover is nothing new. But the Great Resignation and extreme turnover of American workers—white-collar workers and low-wage workers alike—that occurred across industries was a unique phenomenon that no business was prepared for.

Experience It Forward

What your employees experience, your customers will also. The best marketing is happy, engaged employees. It is a certainty: Your customers will never be any happier than your employees. You can build amazing facilities, products, and services; however, it is your people who create and deliver the experience that keeps customers coming back.

> **"It must thrive inside to be experienced outside."**
> **—Joseph Michelli**

A Professional Awakening

For so many, the pandemic was a professional awakening, like people who survive a near-death experience. Employees reevaluated their professional careers, not only in regards to what they wanted, but also what they weren't willing to tolerate anymore. However, too many leaders used the Great Resignation era as a crutch. A significant percentage of people who quit during and post-pandemic did so as a result of poor company culture, with leaders focused solely on productivity and bottom-line profits.

The Two Biggest Mistakes Companies Make

This mass resignation of employees caught many leaders and companies flat-footed. These business leaders panicked and made the two biggest mistakes companies make when attempting to combat a turnover crisis: 1) they quickly filled positions with any person they could find, and 2) they continued to employ poor performers—the ones who merely took up space, dragging down a team's collective energy and frustrating their top talent. This cycle leads inevitably to even more turnover and staff shortages. New employees in these reactive companies got little or no training to do their jobs well.

If the Great Resignation wasn't a big enough issue for leaders to try to navigate and correct, then came Quiet Quitting, a term referring to employees doing the mere minimum of their job description and nothing else. Instead of employees quitting and leaving, many quit and stayed. Growing weary of hustle culture, at least half of the American workforce reportedly joined the Quiet Quitting movement![2]

Supply chain issues were a problem that impacted almost every industry during the pandemic. "Hiring" and "Out of Stock" became two common signs and phrases. Companies caught unprepared for these supply chain and staffing issues often poorly managed their customers' expectations by not being totally transparent and by communicating poorly about delays.

Customers Paying More Yet Receiving Less

Not every company was hurt by the pandemic. Many industries and companies got busier during and/or immediately after the pandemic, hitting record sales.

But from the perspective of the consumer, supply chain issues contributed to the highest inflation in decades. Gas prices and costs for most other consumer goods rose dramatically. Staff and product shortages frustrated customers, who were now paying higher prices even though they were getting significantly less.

Shrinkflation

When brands are faced with the rising costs of production, companies traditionally have two options: raise prices, which could result in a loss of sales; or accept lower margins (profits), which will result in unhappy shareholders when stock prices inevitably fall.

However, a third, self-serving option that many brands choose to apply is the strategy known as "Shrinkflation." Shrinkflation is a form of retail camouflage in which consumers pay more for a growing range of products without realizing it. By shrinking typical item sizes and net weights, companies and businesses aim to cover rising labor and material costs without increasing the prices of their products, while hoping consumer spending will remain at the same level.

This cagey method of value adjustment is particularly reflected in food prices. You may not notice if a bag of chips has five fewer chips or if your roll of paper towels contains fewer sheets.

Manufacturers don't think consumers will realize these seemingly small adjustments. For example, Gatorade reduced their bottle size from 32 to 28 ounces, while charging the same price, which is about a 14 percent price increase. Even packages of Reese's Peanut Butter Cups, beloved by many for decades, have seen a 0.10 ounce decrease in size since the early 2000s.[3]

Other examples of Shrinkflation manifest in the service industry. Some spas advertise a one-hour massage, but actual massage time is only 50 minutes. This reduction also appears in meal serving sizes at restaurants. Shrinkflation is not what we mean when we say build a customer experience that makes price irrelevant. Tricking your customers is not the way you build trust and brand loyalty. It is the exact opposite.

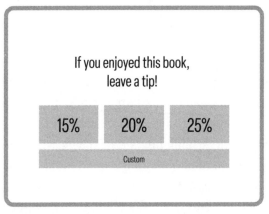

Image 1.2

Has Tipflation Reached a Tipping Point

Yes, I am jumping on the tipping bandwagon. Everyone is doing it. Not only has the average tipping percentage increased dramatically, but who we tip has expanded. It appears more people and businesses are requesting and expecting a tip these days. It doesn't matter if you are picking up an order to go, or a cashier is ringing out items you selected to purchase. The employee spins the iPad around asking us how much we would like to tip. Consumers feel pressured to not only tip, but tip well, with the employee standing there watching. This is known as "guilt-tipping."

Tipflation and tip creep are terms to describe the United States recent widespread expansion of gratuity to more industries, as opposed to being traditionally only prevalent in full-service restaurants.

The most frustrating part is how businesses are trying to put the burden on their customers to providing their employees a livable wage. We no longer reward excellent service with a generous tip. The increase in asking customers to tip is causing a poor customer experience.

DoorDash warns Customers that if they don't tip, their deliveries may take longer

DoorDash is working the "guilt-tipping" movement. Recently DoorDash has started sending out an alert to their customers, who choose not to tip, that says, "Orders with no tip might take longer to get delivered — are you sure you want to continue?"

The app also shares this alert to customers, "Dashers can pick and choose which orders they want to do," says the alert, which refers to its delivery drivers as Dashers. "Orders that take longer to be accepted by Dashers tend to result in a slower delivery."

One DoorDash driver shared with Business Insider that his earnings have plummeted over the past five years and DoorDash pressuring customers to tip has not helped his earnings. Since the announcement of the no-tip warning, he's noticed a drop in tips, he said. "It's pretty crappy that they're turning on us," he said of DoorDash. "I do feel like the customer should tip us a bit better. But at the same time, DoorDash should pay us better."

Earlier this year, DoorDash started sending messages encouraging their customers about tipping their drivers more. These messages told customers that they could increase tips for 30 days after a delivery.

Not All Profit Is Good Profit

When organizations apply shortsighted thinking, focusing solely on sales and profits, they often enact bad-profit policies that exploit customers (think hidden charges, excessive late fees, overdraft fees, flight change fees, etc.). Short-term profit incentives push many companies in the wrong direction. Bonus plans reward executives for boosting short-term profits even if they embrace practices that take advantage of customers and exasperate customer-facing employees, who are the messengers taking the brunt of the customers' frustrations. The truth is most incentive programs hold teams accountable primarily for meeting cost or revenue targets. Whenever profits are squeezed, an organization's tendency is to seek short-term profitable opportunities such as bad-profit policies.

Companies relying heavily on bad profits alienate customers and offer opportunities for emerging brands to capitalize. For example, remember Blockbuster? Back in the early 2000s, Blockbuster wouldn't go to a subscription model because they made $800 million in late fees, or 16 percent of its revenue.[4] Enter Netflix. So long, Blockbuster.

Eradicating Bad Profit

Walt Bettinger found early on in his tenure as CEO of Charles Schwab that one-quarter of Schwab's revenues resulted from bad profits. He asked his team to rank in order the offending policies—putting the worst at the top of the list—and committed the company to working from the top down, eradicating each policy so that within several years they all would be gone. Bettinger realized this practice was essential to creating a customer service culture.[5]

Under Bettinger's leadership, the value of Schwab stock has grown from $13.59 at the beginning of 2009 to around $95.00 in 2022, with market capitalization increasing tenfold. Not surprisingly, the CEO has received numerous awards over the past decade, including *Fortune* magazine's Businessperson of the Year four times, as well as landing in its number seven global businessperson spot. Charles Schwab offers an outstanding example of what can happen when leaders have a true understanding of the customer service experience and structure their policies with a moral compass firmly in place.

Who's to blame for all of this?

Could it be Milton Friedman's fault? American economist Friedman is famous for his theory introduced back in 1970 in an essay for the *New York Times* titled "A Friedman Doctrine,"[6] in which he stated, "There is one and only one social responsibility of business, to use its resources and engage in activities designed to increase its profits to maximize shareholders' wealth."

He argued that a company has no social responsibility to the public or society; its only responsibility is to its shareholders.[7] For his theory, which became extremely influential in the corporate world over the following decades, Friedman was awarded a Nobel Prize.

We would argue Friedman's theory ignited corporate greed and unethical behavior, the effects of which we are still feeling over 50 years later. People like Jack Welch, former CEO of

General Electric, became the poster boy for corporate capitalism; he was obsessed with doing anything to increase GE's stock prices and value, such as laying off massive numbers of workers, which became known as "corporate restructuring." The pressure was on leaders to either hit their numbers or hit the road.

The truth is that despite today's profusion of customer-centric rhetoric, most companies and its leaders still believe and, more importantly, their actions translate that the primary purpose of business is profits.

Greedflation

> "Greed is good. Greed is right. Greed works."
> —Gordon Gekko in *Wall Street*

Contrary to the words of Gordon Gekko, the ruthless character played by Michael Douglas in the movie *Wall Street*, greed leads to unethical behavior. Today, as a society, we seem numb to corporate scandals, such as those of Enron, WeWork, Theranos, Uber, Arthur Andersen, Facebook, Lehman Brothers, and BP. The list goes on and on. When unethical corporate behavior becomes the norm, both employees and customers lose trust in the organization's brands.

However, even if an organization is not behaving illegally, it can still be behaving unethically by being greedy. Greedflation refers to how employee compensation is falling further and further behind relative to senior-level executive pay. The last time the federal minimum wage was increased was in 2009, meaning it has declined by 26 percent from 2009 to 2023. The Economic

Policy Institute (EPI) estimates that CEO compensation has grown 1,460 percent since 1978, while typical worker compensation has risen just 18 percent. In 2021, CEOs of the top 350 firms in the US made $27.8 million, on average—400 times more than a typical worker.[8]

The Great Shareholder-Stakeholder Debate

Stakeholder theory is a more recent theory of business that argues against the separation of economics and ethics. It states that short-term profits—gained by prioritizing shareholders—should not be the primary objective of a business. Here, stakeholders include customers, employees, suppliers, local communities, and more.

Under this theory, prioritizing the needs and interests of stakeholders over shareholders is more likely to lead to long-term success, both for the business and for the communities that it is a part of. This stakeholder mindset is, in turn, likely to create long-term value for both stakeholders and shareholders.

In contrast to Friedman's shareholder theory, Dr. Edward Freeman, professor at Darden School of Business, University of Virginia, and longtime proponent of the stakeholder theory, suggests that a company's stakeholders are "those groups without whose support the organization would cease to exist."[9] This view paints the corporate environment as an ecosystem of related interdependent groups, all of whom need to be considered and satisfied to keep the company healthy and successful in the long term.

"I actually think if Milton Friedman were alive today, I think he would be a stakeholder theorist. I think he would understand that the only way to create value for shareholders in today's world is to pay attention to customers, suppliers, employees, communities, and shareholders at the same time," Freeman says.[10]

The Ending of Shareholder Primacy

In January 2020, the World Economic Forum came out with a manifesto urging companies to move to "stakeholder capitalism." Around the same time, the Business Roundtable (BRT) published a proclamation on "The Purpose of a Corporation": "We share a fundamental commitment to all of our stakeholders." It was signed by 181 CEOs whose companies represented over one-third of the total market capitalization in the US equity markets.[11] As a result, *Fortune* described it as "ending shareholder primacy,"[12] and the *Financial Times* called it "abandoning the shareholder-first mantra."[13]

Now for the Good News

There are several organizations that are focused on building a world-class experience ecosystem for every stakeholder of their business. We have seen firsthand that companies with the strongest internal cultures were significantly less affected by the Great Resignation and Quiet Quitting. And the organizations that churned and burned their team members are the ones now being hit the hardest by employee turnover and economic instability.

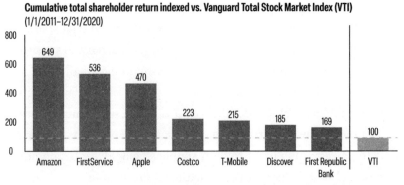

Cumulative total shareholder return indexed vs. Vanguard Total Stock Market Index (VTI)
(1/1/2011–12/31/2020)

Amazon: 649
FirstService: 536
Apple: 470
Costco: 223
T-Mobile: 215
Discover: 185
First Republic Bank: 169
VTI: 100

Image 1.3

How do companies outperform competitors and the stock market by significant margins, in any economy? By being customer experience leaders in their industries. Make no mistake about it, there is a direct correlation between love, loyalty, and profitability. According to Bain & Co., companies achieving the highest net promoter scores (NPS), a customer satisfaction tool, in their industry consistently beat the stock market over the past decade, with annual returns of 26 percent plus.[14] (See Image 1.3.)

Return on Experience

Over the 16-year period from 2005 to 2021, the top customer satisfaction companies across a wide range of industries generated annualized returns of 20.16 percent for the ACSI Leaders portfolio, while the S&P 500 had an annualized return of 10.97 percent. (See Image 1.4.)

Also, Image 1.5 shows a strong correlation between the overall customer satisfaction average and corporate profits over time. Customer satisfaction started to decline around 2013. Average

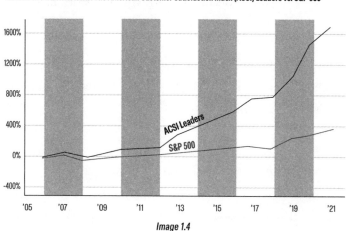

Cumulative Stock Returns: The American Customer Satisfaction Index (ACSI) Leaders vs. S&P 500

Image 1.4

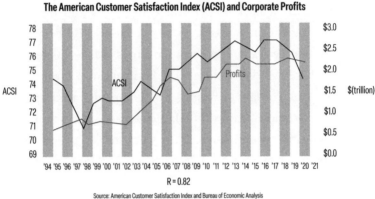

The American Customer Satisfaction Index (ACSI) and Corporate Profits

R = 0.82

Source: American Customer Satisfaction Index and Bureau of Economic Analysis

Image 1.5

corporate profit followed suit. A company's profitability often follows a change in its customer satisfaction.

Claes Fornell, chairman and founder of the American Customer Satisfaction Index, states: "In competitive markets, firms are rewarded by treating their customers well and punished for treating them badly. The rewards/punishments show up, not only in earnings, but also in stock prices and make equity markets better aligned with consumer utility, which, in turn, causes an upward shift in demand curves. As a result, consumer spending increases and so does economic growth. Investors in customer satisfaction don't just beat the market, they also contribute to a stronger economy."[15]

Image 1.6 shows the direct correlation of NPS and stock market values of automakers. The higher the NPS scores, the higher the value of the automaker.

Financial Performance versus Net Promoter Score

In his book *Winning on Purpose*, author Fred Reichheld shares an incredible comparison of two groups of companies.[16] The first

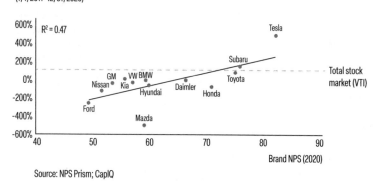

US auto: Customer-love wins

Cumulative total shareholder return (ln)
(1/1/2011–12/31/2020)

Image 1.6

group was comprised of the 11 organizations Jim Collins focused on in his groundbreaking book *Good to Great*, which he identified as "great" based on financial criteria as the only competitive differentiator. These 11 were compared to the NPS leaders featured around the same time in Reichheld's earlier book, *The Ultimate Question 2.0*. (See Image 1.7.)

Bain teams examined the total shareholder return of the 11 "great" companies featured in *Good to Great* for a decade following that book's publication. Bain then performed the same analysis for the NPS leader companies from *The Ultimate Question 2.0* for the decade after that book's release. Then, Bain compared both sets of companies to the median stock market return in the decade following each book's publication.

As you can see in Image 1.8, the *Good to Great* companies delivered only 40 percent of the median market performance, while top-performing NPS organizations delivered 510 percent of the median return. In other words, the firms appearing great through the lens of financial performance made their investors unhappy over the decade, while investors in companies that

Good to Great	The Ultimate Question 2.0–NPS Leaders	
Abbott	Amazon	MetroPCS (now T-Mobile)
Circuit City	American Express	Southwest
Fannie Mae	Apple	State Farm* (Life Ins.)
Gillette	Chick-fil-A*	Symantec (now Norton)
Kimberly-Clark	Costco	Trader Joe's*
Kroger	Facebook	USAA* (P&C Insurance)
Nucor	Google	Vanguard*
Philip Morris	JetBlue	Verizon (Internet)
Pitney Bowes	Kaiser Permanente*	
Walgreens		
Wells Fargo		*Not publicly traded

Image 1.7

Total shareholder return (TSR) vs. US median

Cumulative total shareholder return indexed vs. US public firms (median) for the
decade beginning January 1st of each book's year of publication

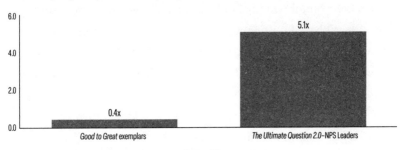

Image 1.8

focused on delighting their customers also delighted their investors in the next decade.

So why did the companies that were labeled "great" in Jim Collins's book not maintain that level? Reichheld explains it this way: "Those firms (like most companies today) gauged their success using the metrics of financial capitalism—primarily profits. When profits become purpose, it becomes too easy for large and powerful firms to boost their financial performance by shortchanging both their customer base, and their employees."[17]

> "The companies that don't invest in customer experience are the ones whose leaders don't understand the financial impact CX can have."

BX Strong

This is why organizations need to focus on being brand eXperience strong (BX strong), which is an entire experience ecosystem of how your organization *intentionally* interacts and treats every one of its stakeholders. The companies that will dominate their industries for the next decade will be the ones obsessed with evolving the experience at every level—employee, customer, vendor, and community. The following chapters will explore arguably the most important piece, the employee experience.

2

WELCOME TO THE EMPLOYEE EXPERIENCE REVOLUTION

"We need to build the type of company that helps employees be their best selves and have an opportunity to live their best lives."

—JOHN DIJULIUS III

John, have a confession to make. As an entrepreneur, terms such as "the Great Resignation," "Quiet Quitting," and "the canceling of hustle culture" really made me angry, at least initially. These terms represent the opposite of everything I have ever known to be the recipe of success. Everything I have ever done in my life to overachieve and get to where I am today. Everything I have ever preached to my sons: Show up early, do more than anyone else, give more in every situation, don't keep score, be loyal, and always play the long game.

I didn't want to be judgmental and jump on the "younger generations are entitled and lazy" bandwagon. I wanted to figure out what the logic was behind all of this, especially the mindset of the younger generations (millennials and Gen Zs). I am by nature an optimist, an idealist. So, I started to research, which included a lot of reading, listening to podcasts, watching videos, and asking many questions. And as with anything explored with an open mind, I started seeing how and why younger employees think and feel the way they do.

Maybe the Younger Generation Gets It, and We Were Wrong

One of John's favorite podcasters, Scott Galloway, writes in a great piece called "Advice to Grads: Be Warriors, Not Wokesters":

> Don't do what you are asked to do, but what you are capable of doing . . . Get strong, really strong. You should be able to walk into a room and believe you could overpower, outrun, or outlast every person in the room . . . take as much of this energy and time for the next couple years and reallocate that human capital to three things: work, relationships, and fitness . . . Balance is a myth. There are only trade-offs. Having balance at my age is a function of lacking it at your age.[1]

We love and agree 100 percent with what Galloway says. Especially this part: "Having balance at my age is a function of lacking it at your age." However, who is to say that is the way everyone should believe or behave? Who is to say that older generations were right?

The younger generation got a front-row seat watching their parents and grandparents work their tails off, all in the hopes of building a better life for their children. They didn't like what they saw. For many of their older family members, all that hard work didn't end up paying off financially. It sometimes included getting laid off or working way past retirement—often up until the day they died. As for the ones for whom it did pay off financially, that, too, came at a cost. The greatest cost, other than regret, was a lack of solid relationships with their spouse, children, and friends. In high achievers it is not uncommon to see patterns of high divorce rates and potential substance abuse struggles.

Younger Generations Say: Take Your Hustle Culture and Shove It

Elon Musk once tweeted, "Nobody ever changed the world on 40 hours a week." However, the millennials and zoomers (Zs) are not willing to trade the hope for advancement in their professional careers at the cost of their personal lives and happiness. Hustle culture, today known as "burnout culture," refers to the mentality that one must work all day, every day in pursuit of one's professional goals. For many, hustle culture becomes a lifestyle, an obsessive drive, which appears as a motivational movement with a pot of gold waiting for you at the end. "Rise and Grind" is both the theme of a Nike ad campaign and the title of a book by a *Shark Tank* shark.[2]

It's Not All That It's Cracked Up to Be

Most employees live paycheck to paycheck, struggling to pay their bills. The nine-to-five workday has become very blurry, especially if an employee wants to be recognized by management and is hoping for a promotion and raise.

Marianne Cooper, a sociologist from Stanford University, described hypercompetitiveness as the idea that both men and women are expected to continually demonstrate their abilities, strive for victory, and prioritize work above all other aspects of life.[3]

Workaholism

Society has conditioned us to believe that anyone can achieve anything if they work hard enough. The term "workaholism" refers to a go-getter who is celebrated for putting in 12-plus-hour workdays and wearing it like a badge of honor, shaming those who do not do the same. What isn't explained is, at what cost? "The vast majority of people beating the drum of hustle-mania are not the people doing the actual work. They're the managers, financiers and owners," says David Heinemeier Hansson, one of the authors of *It Doesn't Have to Be Crazy at Work*, a book about creating healthy company cultures.[4] Today, people want more meaning in their lives. The pandemic was a professional awakening, prompting employees to take a pause and reflect on this hustle lifestyle. The realization was that hustle culture can be disruptive to mental and physical well-being. Consequently, many have chosen to opt out.

In an article titled "Millennials Cancel Hustle Culture," K. Badar shares, "The pandemic helped people across the world realize the importance of genuine social connections. Locked in, they rediscovered their families and friends. They were able to take their mind off from their work and contemplate what the world truly was. They understood the value of free time."[5] April Wilson, MD, chair of the preventive medicine department at Loma Linda University Health in California, says "hustle culture is about being a 'human doing' rather than a 'human being.'"[6]

Quit Rate

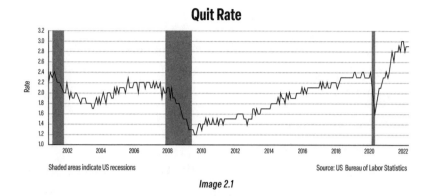

Shaded areas indicate US recessions   Source: US Bureau of Labor Statistics

Image 2.1

Work to Live, or Live to Work

All of this has led many employees to join the Great Resignation and Quiet Quitting movements. The *New York Post* reports that 42 percent of Gen Zs would rather be at a company that gives them a sense of purpose than one that pays more, compared to 40 percent of millennials and 32 percent of Gen Xers who said the same.[7]

Great Resignation Started Long Before Most Realize

The Great Resignation, also called the "Big Quit," refers to the employees who voluntarily quit their companies at higher-than-usual rates during the COVID-19 pandemic (2020–2022). However, these employee resignations began a decade or more earlier. Research reveals that the quit rate started to climb in 2009 and steadily kept rising and gaining momentum for the next ten-plus years.[8] (See Image 2.1.)

The Top Reasons for Why People Quit

According to surveys created by the Pew Research Center, the top three reasons why employees quit their jobs are:

1. Low pay (63 percent)

2. No opportunities for advancement (63 percent)

3. Feeling disrespected at work (57 percent)[9]

Unrewarded Loyalty

For many experienced employees, the Great Resignation paid off. According to a 2023 Pew Research Center report, 60 percent of people saw an increase in real earnings after they switched employers, compared with 47 percent of those who remained in the same job.[10] Another way to look at it, when you factor in cost of living, is that the average employee who quit and got a new job enjoyed an increase in pay, while the average worker who stayed in place saw a loss during the April 2021 to March 2022 period. (See Image 2.2.) Clearly, every organization needs to have a solid employee retention strategy in place.

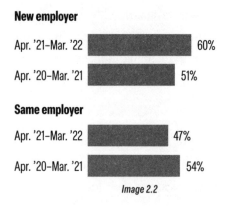

A rising share of workers who changed jobs are earning more as a result

% of US workers who saw a real wage increase over the same month a year earlier (12-month average)

New employer

Apr. '21–Mar. '22   60%

Apr. '20–Mar. '21   51%

Same employer

Apr. '21–Mar. '22   47%

Apr. '20–Mar. '21   54%

Image 2.2

Quiet Quitting

The pandemic changed the way much of America works. A major consequence of the work-from-home (WFH) era is that a significant percentage of the employees who haven't joined the Great Resignation bandwagon are disengaged and reluctant to go beyond their regular work hours and duties—a response mentioned earlier, known as Quiet Quitting. A Gallup survey found that half of employees are "not engaged" at work and another 18 percent are "actively disengaged." The proportion of employees who are engaged compared to those who are actively disengaged reached a ratio of 1.8 to 1, marking its lowest point in nearly a decade.[11] (See Image 2.3.)

Another contributing factor to Quiet Quitting is the result of being away from colleagues and the office. Employers struggle with maintaining a strong corporate culture that makes employees feel part of something larger than themselves. Proximity leads to connectivity. Strong emotional connection to your team is difficult to replicate over Zoom. Quiet Quitting is employees sending a wake-up call to leaders to build better, more rewarding company cultures.

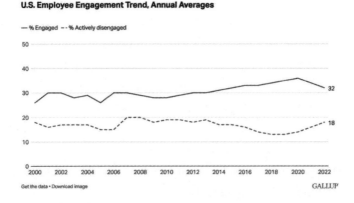

Image 2.3: Unengaged employees are like squatters taking up space in your organization.

Your Biggest Expense Is Dissatisfied Employees

A new study from the University of Houston joins a growing body of research findings that conclude that job satisfaction has a lot more to do with the people we work with than it does with the actual work we do.[12] And Gallup data tells us that businesses with the highest employee engagement, compared to companies with the lowest engagement, benefit from:

- 18 percent more productivity
- 23 percent more profitability
- 81 percent less absenteeism
- 43 percent less turnover[13]

What makes for a fulfilling life?

What do you think is the top thing people say makes their life most fulfilling? A great life partner? Raising kids? Money? The Pew Research Center conducted a study to better understand Americans' views of factors that lead to a fulfilling life. Surprisingly, the majority surveyed said job satisfaction was the most important, followed by friendship. Even more surprising was how marriage and being a parent fell behind. A significant 71 percent of adults emphasized the extreme or very high importance of having an enjoyable job or career for a fulfilling life. Additionally, 61 percent placed an equal level of importance on having close friends. In contrast, only around one in four adults considered having children (26 percent) or being married (23 percent) as extremely or very important factors for achieving a fulfilling life.[14] (See Image 2.4.)

Americans see jobs and close friends, rather than marriage and parenthood, as highly important elements in living a fulfilling life

% saying, in general, each of the following is ___ important in order to live a fulfilling life

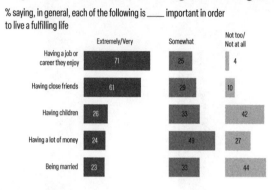

Note: Share of respondents who didn't offer an answer are not shown.
Source: Survey of US adults conducted April 10–16, 2023.

Image 2.4

The Correlation between Happiness at Work and Overall Life Satisfaction

Caring for your employees impacts their professional lives as well as the company's bottom line. It is impossible to separate one's professional life from their personal life. If an employee is miserable at their job and works in a toxic environment, their overall happiness will be impacted.

"When it comes to employee happiness, bosses and supervisors play a bigger role than one might guess. Relationships with management is the top factor in employees' job satisfaction, which in turn is the second most important determinant of employees' overall well-being. According to our analysis, only mental health is more important for overall life satisfaction," share the authors in McKinsey & Company's article, "The Boss Factor: Making the World a Better Place Through Workplace Relationships."[15] (See Image 2.5.)

Relationships with management is a critical factor in employees' life satisfaction.
Share of satisfaction explained by each factor,[1] %

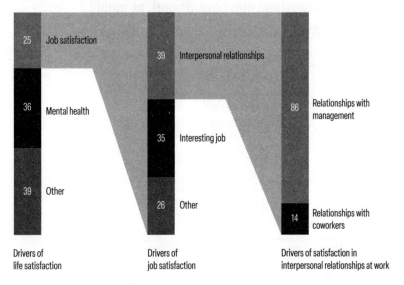

Drivers of
life satisfaction

Drivers of
job satisfaction

Drivers of satisfaction in
interpersonal relationships at work

[1] Drivers of life satisfaction based on various UK and European surveys; drivers of job satisfaction and satisfaction in interpersonal relationships based on a 2015 International Social Survey Programme Work Orientations module (n = 27,732 respondents across 37 countries).

Source: Jan-Emmanuel De Neve et al., "Work and well-being: A global perspective," *Global Happiness Policy Report 2018*, February 10, 2018, happinesscouncil.org; Richard Layard, *Can We Be Happier?: Evidence and Ethics* (London, UK: Pelican Books, 2020); McKinsey analysis

Image 2.5

It Always Starts at the Top

Unfortunately, research also shows 75 percent of employees say that the most stressful aspect of their job is their immediate boss.[16]

"Senior leaders can create a step change in both shareholder and social value by clearly articulating the sizable upsides to high job satisfaction, including educating managers on their pivotal roles and embedding quality of workplace relationships into manager development and performance appraisals. They can also act as critical change agents by embracing servant leadership and approaching everyone in their organization with compassion and genuine curiosity," state Tera Allas and Bill Schaninger, authors of the McKinsey article.[17]

Employees' satisfaction is positively correlated with several aspects of company performance, including shareholder value.

Correlation between employee satisfaction and selected performance metrics[1]

Annual shareholder returns for 100 best companies to work for ("Top 100"), relative to given portfolio, 1998–2009,[2] %

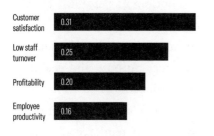

Customer satisfaction	0.31
Low staff turnover	0.25
Profitability	0.20
Employee productivity	0.16

Top 100 returns in excess of risk-free portfolio	+3.5%
Top 100 returns in excess of portfolio of similar companies	+2.1%
Top 100 returns in excess of portfolio of companies with similar characteristics	+1.8%

[1] Meta-analysis combining observations from >1.8 million employees and 82,000 business units.
[2] Risk adjusted; based on list compiled by *Fortune* for the United States

Source: Jan-Emmanuel De Neve, Christian Krekel, and George Ward, *Employee Wellbeing, Productivity and Firm Performance*, CEP discussion paper, number 1605, March 2019, cep.lse.ac.uk; Jan-Emmanuel De Neve et al., "Work and well-being: A global perspective," *Global Happiness Policy Report 2018*, February 10, 2018, happinesscouncil.org; Alex Edmans, "Does the stock market fully value intangibles? Employee satisfaction and equity prices," *Journal of Financial Economics*, September 2011, Volume 101, Number 3, pp. 621–40; McKinsey analysis

Image 2.6

A strong leader instills a sense of caring, trust, and confidence in their team members. Love and trust can't be demanded; they must be given to be received. In these types of cultures, employees feel empowered and are more likely to give feedback on how things can be better. When employees are part of the innovation process, an incredible sense of ownership and buy-in occurs, as well as a significant increase in execution.

Leaders Work in the Employee Perception Business

Countless studies show irrefutable evidence correlating employee satisfaction, customer loyalty, and profitability. For example, one study showed how call center workers' weekly sales increased by 25 percent when their happiness increased by one point (on a scale of 1 to 5).[18] Other research found in the *Journal of Applied*

Psychology, titled "Business-Unit-Level Relationship between Employee Satisfaction, Employee Engagement, and Business Outcomes," found that the top 25 percent of brands with the highest employee engagement enjoyed one to four percentage points higher profit margins than those in the bottom 25 percent.[19] That should satisfy the shareholder theorists. (See Image 2.6.)

The primary duty of leaders is to care for their people. They must inspire teams to embrace a customer purpose and enable their success by allocating sufficient time, education, and resources to accomplish this mission. Leaders must role model, practice, preach, and teach the values that systematically reinforce a loving culture through symbols, words, and deeds.

> **"Leading people is a privilege and a responsibility, and it is not exploitable. You have to earn this privilege."**

Leadership Epiphany on Workplace Culture

"You are the average of the five people you spend the most time with." You have probably heard this quote hundreds of times. John admits to repeating it hundreds of times to his own three boys, at new employee orientations, and to any young person who asks him for advice.

The point of this quote is that each of us is the one responsible for who we allow in our inner circle of friends, who we allow to influence our thoughts, behaviors, and actions. We must, therefore, audit the people we surround ourselves with, making sure that we do our best to only spend time with people who make us better, inspire us, and encourage us in all areas of our lives.

Our leadership epiphany was that our employees do not get

to choose who they work with, the people they spend more time with than they do their family and friends. As leaders, we are the ones who choose for them.

Employees Don't Quit Companies, They Quit . . .

You most likely finished the above sentence with the word "leaders." We somewhat disagree with this adage. This is only partly true. The more correct and complete way to say it is, "Employees don't quit companies, they quit people." Employees quit because of the people they work with (coworkers) and for (leaders).

When rock stars are surrounded by coworkers who are poor performers with bad attitudes, one of two things will happen: 1) our rock stars are going to get the hell out of there and find a new company to work for; high performers hate working with poor performers. Or, 2) your rock stars will gravitate to the average of their coworkers and no longer be high performers.

When leaders compromise on who they hire and who they allow to stay, they are polluting their employees' workplace culture. As a leader, you are responsible for the average of the five team members your employees spend the most time with.

> **"You can't hire your way out of a bad culture."**

As Leaders, We Need to Do Better; Employees Deserve Better

The "Great Resignation," "Quiet Quitting," and "Cancel Culture" are not indictments on employees, but rather business leaders' lack of focus on truly caring for the people who are under their command. Today, employees are more selective than ever regarding who they will work for; they are insisting that companies and their leaders help them live the right life.

In his book *The Excellence Dividend*, Tom Peters writes, "Leading is the pinnacle of human achievement. Your #1 task is helping others grow and develop and contribute to their colleagues and communities. Your accomplishment list will be measured by those who went on to be wildly successful in large measure because of the time spent with you."[20]

Most of the world's population cannot avoid working during their lifetime. Therefore, it is essential that they find meaning and value in what they do and who they do it for. We only have one life to live. We do not have a professional life and a personal life. It is one life. And if we don't like what we do, it will be hard to live a meaningful life.

> "We need to build organizations that give every human being the opportunity to thrive. Every person needs something in their life that ignites their passion, something that captivates and energizes them."
> —Gary Hamel and Michele Zanini, authors of *Humanocracy*

We really like what Jim Clifton, the chairman of Gallup, says: "The real foundation of a life well lived is, if you are going to have to work, you need to work someplace and do something that you think is important and makes the world a better place; otherwise it means your life didn't matter. Going to work needs to be a rich experience if you want to have a great life on earth."[21]

In his famous commencement speech at Stanford, Steve Jobs gave the graduates great advice: "You've got to find what you love. Your work is going to fill a large part of your life, and the only way to be truly satisfied is to do what you believe is great work. And the only way to do great work is to love what you do. If you haven't found it yet, keep looking. Don't settle."[22]

> **"Stop trying to find great employees; focus on becoming the business great employees find."**

The market is being flooded with people looking for something better, people who have had enough of organizations that do not care about them as human beings. For those business leaders who take the time and energy to not only talk about being better but prove that they lead a better, more caring place to work, there is a tremendous pool of talent waiting to beat a path to their door.

Weaponize Adversity

Crisis creates opportunity. A crisis is a horrible thing to waste! As business owners, we prefer recessionary times or even the Great Resignation. It isn't that any of our businesses do better in such times, but that our competition does worse. During difficult business conditions, your business has an incredible opportunity to lap your competitors—to totally crush them, gain more market share, have the pick of the top talent, and maybe even enjoy record profits.

> **"You may own the business, but you just rent the people."**

While it seems no industry dodged the Great Resignation, it is safe to say that companies most impacted by the big reshuffle were ones that could not function without on-site employees. Restaurants, hotels, health care, retail, and fitness clubs all became less attractive to employees because working from home (WFH) was not an option in those types of industries. Yet some brands from these industries found ways to weaponize this adversity. How? Long before the pandemic, they were obsessed with creating the type of culture employees wanted to be part of, even if that meant not having the WFH option.

There is a reason why Self Esteem Brands, parent company to Anytime Fitness, Waxing the City, The Bar Method, and Basecamp Fitness, is repeatedly ranked one of the top places to work. They operate in nearly 40 countries on seven continents and have more than three million members worldwide. The culture starts in the DNA of founders Chuck Runyon and David Mortensen and their obsession for building a work culture that employees truly love, one that goes far beyond work-life balance and results in a healthier workforce.

"Most business leaders hated The Great Resignation. I love it," says Runyon. "People should have leverage and work where they want to work."[23] Runyon believes that since employees get to choose their jobs, they should love them, and that employers are responsible for creating jobs their employees will love.

Runyon doesn't buy what many leaders use as a crutch, that our workforce is lazy or doesn't want to work anymore. "The great misinterpretation of The Great Resignation is that people have unrealistic expectations. Contrary to what bad bosses think, employees want to work hard."[24] Purpose and connection matter to quality talent, something both current employers and those seeking new employees must keep in mind for greater retention of staff.

Self Esteem Brands' two cofounders, Runyon and Mortensen, wrote the book *Love Work*,[25] which is based on the pillars they have built their amazing culture around, the 4 Ps: people, purpose, profits, and play. Their obsession with building a world-class internal culture has more than paid off.

The Great Inspiration

"As employers, we have a golden opportunity to transform The Great Resignation into The Great Inspiration. Especially after the two years [of the pandemic], people don't just want to be paid—they want to be inspired. So let's inspire them," preaches Runyon.[26]

Self Esteem Brands offers to pay for their employees and their families to access mental health experts through Modern Health.[27] Every Friday in the summer is a non-working Wellbeing Friday. They encourage No Meeting Wednesdays, which frees up time for their team members to focus and dive into their roles. They offer unlimited PTO. Such resources for staff can only add up to better emotional health for the company's employees.

Runyon and Mortensen have made it their life mission to inspire their employees. Anytime Fitness is now the world's largest co-ed fitness club franchise, reaching a bigger international market penetration more quickly than any franchise in history. More impressively, the Anytime Fitness logo has been tattooed on the bodies of more than 5,000 employees, franchisees, and customers—a symbol of passion most brands can only dream of.

"Our purpose is to improve the self-esteem of the world—something we can only achieve through a workplace culture that provides the means for our people to put their own health and wellness front and center," says Runyon.[28]

A great survey question to ask your employees is, "On average, how excited are you to work each day?" Do your employees jump out of bed in the morning and look forward to working, or do they have to hit the snooze button five times and chug a 20-ounce latte just to face the day? The sad truth is most people live in the second category, on default mode. When it comes to work, nearly 70 percent of Americans are disengaged from their professional lives.[29]

Tying in the Customer Service Revolution to the Employee Experience Revolution

The DiJulius Group (TDG), headquartered in Cleveland, Ohio, is a consulting firm that helps organizations build a world-class experience. TDG's purpose is "to change the world by creating a customer service revolution." In fact, in John's book, *The Customer Service Revolution*, Customer Service Revolution (CSR) is defined as:

> A radical overthrow of conventional business mentality designed to transform what employees and customers experience. This shift produces a culture that permeates into people's personal lives, at home, and in the community, which in turn provides the business with higher sales, morale, and brand loyalty—making price irrelevant.[30]

As you can see by the words in bold below, the Employee Experience Revolution is represented in the CSR definition:

> A radical overthrow of conventional business mentality designed to transform what **employees** and customers

experience. **This shift produces a culture that permeates into people's personal lives, at home, and in the community,** which in turn provides the business with higher sales, morale, and **brand loyalty**—making price irrelevant.[31]

To be a great brand, a business must build products and services that improve people's lives. However, it can't stop there. It also must have a major, positive impact on its employees' lives.

The Employee Experience Revolution

Here is how we specifically define the Employee Experience Revolution:

> Great companies help people live extraordinary lives. Their leaders inspire employees to build lives of meaning and purpose.

The following chapters will go into detail on how you can start an Employee Experience Revolution in your own organization. They detail how everything you do has to be an experience, from recruiting to onboarding to maintaining a strong employee experience for your seasoned team members.

Employee eXperience Executive Academy

Back in 2016, due to the rapid growth of the chief customer officer and chief experience officer positions in businesses today, the DiJulius Group created the Customer eXperience Executive Academy (CXEA.org), so companies from all over the world could send their customer experience leaders for comprehensive training and certification on all the facets and responsibilities that fall under customer experience.

Similarly, today, due to an increasing number of companies focusing on the employee experience, the DiJulius Group created the Employee eXperience Executive Academy (EXEA.org). This academy helps leaders, recruiters, and human resource managers build an employee experience, from the interview process to retirement, that focuses on organizations being the best professional decision employees can make.

Welcome to the Employee Experience Revolution!

3

THE POWER OF PURPOSE

"Great leaders make the world a better place; they are willing to do what it takes, make the necessary sacrifices, and rally others to do the same."

—JOHN DIJULIUS III

The Critical Importance Our Work Plays in Our Meaning and Purpose

A study of Shell Oil employees found that those who retired at 55 and lived to be 65 died 37 percent sooner than those who retired at 65. And in general, people who retire at 55 are 89 percent more likely to die within ten years than those who retire at 65. Men who retire at 62 have a 20 percent higher likelihood of death than the general population. These statistics are alarming. It does show how important the role our professional careers play in our sense of purpose and mortality.[1]

The Currency for Younger Generations Is Purpose

It's true that millennials and Gen Zers pose unique challenges for businesses. Companies need to understand what motivates these younger adults. Leaders love to complain about how difficult it is to employ these generations, blaming them for poor customer service—which is funny because a significant percentage of these leaders are the ones who raised them.

John's experience as an employer has been the opposite. He has found in The DiJulius Group, John Robert's Spa, and Believe in Dreams, where we have a large percentage of millennials and Gen Z employees, that this group delivers outstanding customer service consistently. In many cases, they are better at delivering genuine hospitality than older generations who grew up with less technology and therefore had more face-to-face human interactions.

In a survey conducted by Bentley University, 84 percent of millennials said that making a positive difference in the world is more important to them than professional recognition.[2] Similarly, in a study by the Society for Human Resource Management, 94 percent of millennials said they want to use their skills to benefit a cause.[3]

Why do some companies have a large, unmotivated, and apathetic workforce, while other excellent companies boast a workforce willing to make ridiculous sacrifices to achieve insane customer loyalty? One answer may be that they select better candidates (see chapter 4). However, we truly believe only a small fraction of people are born with "service DNA." Great companies with great leaders build a strong, uncompromising culture that is responsible for creating an engaged workforce.

When it comes to the younger generations, it's important to know they're not interested in trading hours for dollars. They want to be part of something big, part of a purpose. Think of companies like Chick-fil-A, Apple, The Ritz-Carlton, Apple, Chewy, Starbucks, and Disney. All these companies employ the dreaded millennials and Zs, yet at these brands, they are fully engaged in their work. The businesses that tie job responsibilities to an overall purpose and a bigger vision get incredible results from these generations—and also from the rest of their employees.

> "People work hard for a paycheck, they work harder for a good boss, and they work hardest for a meaningful purpose. This happens when team members feel that their work enhances the quality of lives around them."

Do Not Underestimate the Power of a Purpose

> "Each of us, truly, has been built to make history."
> —Robin Sharma, author

Think about the most selfless, most sacrificing people you have ever come across. In our experience, these people are volunteers and student athletes, and are involved in charities and political campaigns. In these roles, they make little or no money, and in a lot of cases, it is highly unlikely they can ever make a living in these fields. However, they are part of a cause, part of something bigger. They are focused on their direct impact, and they have an abundance of pride and loyalty to their team. They are part of a special fraternity that they are willing to fight for.

Now think of the top employee experience organizations that have revolutionized stale industries with a completely new model, energized by a workforce on a mission with a promise to provide a truly unique experience. They create the same sense of purpose that volunteer groups, charities, political campaigns, and scholastic sports have. However, they do one thing better: They pay their team members. A purpose and a paycheck.

How to Make Every Team Member Understand How Their Job Impacts Customers' Lives

In most businesses, customer-facing employees typically get the recognition and glory. These include account executives, IT techs, consultants, doctors, lawyers, and accountants. However, those we refer to as invisible service providers—support teams, admins, receptionists, contact center employees, warehouse workers, and back office employees—are rarely praised for the part they play in the customer experience. Yet for the highest levels of employee engagement and job satisfaction, it's crucial that business leaders make every team member understand how their job impacts customers' lives.

Regardless of their position, whether as a customer-facing employee or working behind the scenes, every human being wants to know their hard work is contributing toward something impactful that goes beyond business outcomes. Ignoring this fact is one of the biggest mistakes companies make. All employees tend to thrive on meaningful feedback, sometimes even more than monetary rewards, and their dedication (or lack thereof) strongly impacts the overall quality of customer experience and company reputation. "People want to be part of something larger than themselves. They want to be part of something they are proud of, that they'll fight for, sacrifice for, that they trust," says Howard Schultz, former president and CEO of Starbucks.[4] Clearly, the feeling of making a difference is a key part of a positive work culture.

We have worked with all types of companies from all types of industries, but probably no phone call ever surprised John more than one from A-T Solutions, headquartered in Fredericksburg, Virginia. A-T stands for "anti-terrorism" training and consulting. John was positive that this company, run by ex-military personnel, mistook the title of his first book, *Secret Service*. However, he soon realized that the owner, Ken Falke, was well aware of what John's version of secret service was and was quite serious about making A-T Solutions a world-class customer experience organization. A-T was experiencing enormous growth. Like any other company, leadership realized growth can be difficult when you are trying to get hundreds of employees, including front-facing customer service representatives and project teams, to buy into your organization's philosophy.

One of our projects was to help tie all their departments together and demonstrate how all people across the entire A-T organization—receptionists, salespeople, trainers, human resources, marketing, accounting personnel—contributed to the overall purpose and upheld the core values of the company. Each employee needed to realize that no matter what their specific role, they all worked in customer experience.

As far as employee experiences go, being a receptionist of an anti-terrorist training company probably isn't the sexiest job in the world. So, during one of our workshops, we showed a picture of an A-T Solutions trainer conducting a typical training program with military personnel; we then flashed to a picture of a soldier deployed in Afghanistan. Next, we showed a picture of a soldier stepping off a plane, being greeted by his wife and nine-month-old son, whom he had never met. Finally, we followed that photo with a family vacationing on a beach somewhere. These were powerful images. A-T Solutions doesn't "sell" anti-terrorist training. As a result of what they provide, soldiers come home safely to their families and Americans travel safely together without a second thought of danger or fear. The company's high level of customer service performance makes these things possible. And now, despite limited customer interaction, the receptionist can be proud because she sees the part she plays in the underlying purpose of what A-T Solutions provides.[5]

What We Do Today Impacts Our Customers' Lives

In his book *Built to Serve*, Dan Sanders shares a great example of behind-the-scenes employees who realize they are serving customers. Medtronic is a leader in medical technology, manufacturing prosthetic valves for use in heart surgery. Shift workers spend long hours on assembly lines producing these valves. On the surface, putting pieces and parts together into a box and shipping it off does not appear to be the most rewarding job, nor does it seem directly related to providing excellent customer service. However, Medtronic employees do not see themselves as producing heart valves; rather, they genuinely believe they are helping save lives. Their approach to quality, metaphorically speaking, includes putting their own hearts into their work.

Medtronic holds an annual event where employees can meet patients who are alive because of transplanted artificial hearts containing Medtronic technology. These emotional connections with the end users of their work, the patients, resonate with Medtronic workers. End users share stories with Medtronic employees such as how they were able to walk their daughter down the aisle at her wedding because of the attention to detail Medtronic employees had in their jobs. Talk about a boost in employee morale, not to mention customer service motivation! It is a remarkable illustration of a company applying emotional intelligence to its organizational goals, in a way that will directly impact customer care. Bringing customer support representatives and other employees face-to-face with the people who so greatly benefit from their efforts allows Medtronic to provide a context of higher purpose for its workforce. Such interactions with customers result in focused and fulfilled employees, as company values become team values.[6]

In *The Experience Maker*, John's friend and author Dan Gingiss shares an excellent example of how leaders at Motorola motivate their employees. "Motorola Solutions is a telecommunications equipment provider that largely sells to other businesses and municipal or government units like public safety [it is no longer related to the smartphone manufacturer]," Gingiss writes. "Its products aren't sexy, but they are critical and often lifesaving." He points out that many business-to-business (B2B) marketers feel at a disadvantage to those at business-to-consumer (B2C) companies whose products or services can be advertised in a more exciting way. However, "Motorola Solutions proved this theory wrong with a fantastic video that didn't feature its products so much as it featured the outcomes that its products provide.[7] The video, titled "Moments that Matter," shows police officers, firefighters, teachers, and medical professionals using Motorola Solutions equipment in their daily jobs and achieving extraordinary results."[8] More than just potentially disgruntled customers, these are people for whom experiencing bad customer service or unresolved customer issues could mean the difference between life and death.

By showcasing extraordinary solutions to common issues—particularly ones impacting physical and psychological safety—Motorola is clear about its company goals, promising excellent service that will meet and even exceed customer expectations and undoubtedly have a major impact on the company's customer satisfaction score.

Gingiss concludes, "The video is extraordinary because it isn't just a moving catalog of products; in fact, there isn't a single product mentioned in the entire ad. But it shows the impact of

Motorola Solutions products in an emotional and evocative way. That's hard to do in the B2B world, but certainly not impossible."[9]

The Day Maker Dopamine

Think about the last time you made someone's day. It could have been something so simple but clearly a surprising wow moment for the other person that left a positive impression on them. Yet, at the end of the day, who feels the best? The day maker does.

That is what the top world-class experience brands do: They build, encourage, recognize, and give the resources that allow their employees to constantly go above and beyond, which is why they end up having significantly higher employee fulfillment.

We like to call it the day maker dopamine, which refers to a phenomenon often discussed in psychology and neuroscience. Engaging in acts of kindness or altruism can lead to a release of dopamine, a neurotransmitter associated with pleasure and reward.[10]

This effect has been referred to as a "helper's high" and has been studied in the context of why people feel good when they help others. The idea is that engaging in altruistic behavior activates the reward centers in the brain, leading to the release of dopamine, which in turn creates a feeling of pleasure or satisfaction.

How to Wow

The ability to go above and beyond for customers and coworkers allows your employees to put their fingerprint on the experience. This fosters creative autonomy, allowing employees to come up with their own ideas, to think creatively, to exercise their brains in a new way, giving them a sense of ownership in the experiences they provide. Employees are more connected to the experience they are providing when they feel they have a hand in creating it. Leaders need to make employees feel safe to always do the right thing.

Best of all, employees who perform an act of kindness experience an increase in oxytocin, the chemical that makes us feel warm and fuzzy.[11] Oxytocin is released even when you hear a story of generosity or witness one. The feeling makes us want to be more generous. That is why storytelling and sharing all the great things your team members do for customers and each other is so important.

Organizations achieve greatness when employees are allowed to do unexpected acts, show initiative, exhibit creativity, and step outside the norm. That is when delightful, interesting, and amazing results occur.

> "Let's go make some history, stuff they will talk about for decades that may end up being written about in books, redefining the way things are currently being done."

Us Against the World

As companies grow and mature, most lose their start-up mentality that made them so unique, the "us against the world" underdog mentality. Senior leadership can't understand why, years later, when they have the resources to pay their employees better and offer great benefits and more career opportunities, their new generation of employees are not nearly as committed, loyal, or hardworking as the first few generations.

Why? Because people want to be part of something bigger than themselves, something to fight for. That start-up mentality helped galvanize the first few generations of employees to rally together and fight the Goliaths, to right what was wrong in the world. Typically, these earlier generations of employees gave up better-paying jobs at the time, worked longer hours, and made sacrifices to help the founders make their vision a reality.

Employees went from helping a start-up underdog, flying by the seat of their pants, trying to keep the doors open, to a successful corporation, to now working for that same organization that now has systems, processes, policies, and layers and layers of bureaucracy and management. Back in the day, it was one team. Initial employees would work all weekend with the founders, eating pizza on the floor trying to figure out how they were going to make it. Years later, entry-level employees, maybe even mid-level leaders don't even know the founder/CEO or even have that type of relationship with their direct leader.

The key to scaling successfully is finding ways to maintain that underdog attitude at every stage of your company's life, to keep every generation of employees fighting for your cause, which when done correctly becomes their cause. There is a reason why everyone roots for the heavy underdog team that the pundits give no chance to win.

> **"If you can persuade, inspire, and ignite the imagination of others, you will be unstoppable, irresistible, and irreplaceable."**
> **—Carmine Gallo, author**

Your team members need to believe that the more successful the company is, the better off the world will be. An organization's emotional commitment translates into making company success a personal crusade.

Villain, Victim, Hero

A great way to rally a team around a unified vision is through constantly incorporating the villain, victim, and hero characters into your storytelling. Every great fairy tale, story, book, and movie always possesses three components: a villain, a victim, and a hero.

The villain is the antagonist that needs to be stopped and conquered for the overall good. The villain can be the norm of your industry, dominant companies, the current circumstances, or having no better alternatives. Having an identifiable enemy gives us the chance not only to articulate and showcase our faith, but also to unite ourselves with our fellow believers . . . this us-versus-them strategy attracts people with a common purpose.

The victims are typically innocent and helpless. They are forced into a situation undeservingly and at no fault of their own. They could be the employees of the business, customers, family members, or the community.

The hero is the answer to all the problems and the best solution to stopping the villain. The hero is not one single person but a team, rallying together to be a positive force of good and change. The hero offers a better way of doing something, breaks from the status quo, and inspires people to embrace and accomplish the impossible.

More Is Caught Than Is Taught

Every internal meeting should always open and/or close with your company's *why*, which comes from your mission, purpose, values, and customer experience action statement. You can never tell your team members too often what your brand stands for, how this makes your company different and superior, and the integral role each team member plays in making that a reality.

However, just talking about your values is not enough. Leaders need to model these behaviors 100 percent of the time. Walk the talk, be the example, and constantly share examples of employees who are modeling your values. Great leaders inspire others by the way they live. Your actions demonstrate what your true priorities are more than any words you use. The loudest message you can speak is the way you live your life.

> **"Go show the proper way, and when necessary, use words."**

Who Wants to Be a Billionaire?

From the moment we heard what the new definition of being a billionaire is, we absolutely loved it. It ties in perfectly with creating an Employee Experience Revolution. In his TED Talk, corporate futurist Pete Dulcamara redefined the meaning of billionaire as "someone who positively affects the lives of a billion people."[12]

Each of us absolutely has the ability to be a billionaire. Most of us probably don't come in contact with a billion people in our lifetimes. However, through the hundreds of thousands of people we do encounter—family, friends, employees, coworkers, clients, and strangers—we can practice being kind, genuine, and present. The ripple effect from those positive interactions can positively impact a billion people.

"It's time we create businesses with purpose, businesses that drive humanity-centric innovation. It's time that we stop working for business and business starts to work for us," says Dulcamara.[13] The following chapters will give countless more examples of how great leaders incorporate the power of purpose in their leadership style.

4

CREATING A RECRUITMENT EXPERIENCE

"A just cause is a vision of the future that does not yet exist. And you will commit all your energies to advance that vision. And the people you want to attract believe in your vision of your future. So much so they may turn down a better opportunity somewhere else, because they want to be around people who are committed to building a world that doesn't exist."

—SIMON SINEK, AUTHOR

So many businesses appear desperate when they are understaffed, making them less attractive to top talent. Most companies hire reactively, racing to fill openings caused by either turnover or growth. When companies hire after they have a need instead of before, their objectivity is distorted, and their hiring standards become compromised.

> **"The brands that will survive the next decade will be the ones that remained relentless with their hiring standards."**

It Is Better to Lose the Sale Than the Reputation

Losing the sale is difficult for any entrepreneur or senior leader. As leaders of businesses, we all want sales growth. It is our oxygen, it is what we strive for, strategize for. It is what most of our incentives are based on. However, anytime you allow a less than excellent employee or untrained rookie to serve a customer in order to capitalize on the sale, you compromise the experience you provide to your client and will lose sales in the long run. You will never recover from the poor reputation or the impression that client now has about doing business with you. You will lose the client, and worse, the brand assassination that customer does will deter potential customers from doing business with you.

Too many companies try to solve staff shortages by hiring people as fast as they can just to fill positions, and they also keep employees with bad attitudes. But in any job market, the cost for employee turnover is high: Replacing exiting workers costs one half to two times the employee's annual salary, according to Gallup's "State of the Global Workplace."[1] The cost is borne not only in time spent recruiting, screening, and training new employees, but in employee morale, lack of consistency in customer experience, and existing team members questioning their decision to stay.

The number one priority for businesses today needs to be focusing on keeping their top talent by improving their internal culture. Stop trying to find great employees; instead, focus on becoming the type of business great employees find.

One Bad Employee Can Spread like a
Virus in Even a Healthy Culture

The age-old proverb "One bad apple spoils the barrel" serves as a perfect metaphor for workplace culture. We found the results of the following experiment to be another aha leadership moment, similar to the leadership epiphany we shared in chapter 2 about how our employees are the average of the five people we surround them with.

Will Felps, a professor at Rotterdam School of Management in the Netherlands, conducted a fascinating study demonstrating contagious behavior in the work environment. He split his college students into groups of four and instructed each team to complete a management objective. Teams performing the best would receive a hundred dollars each. What the students didn't know was that the professor included an actor on some of the teams. These actors played one of three roles: a "slacker" who would disengage, put his feet up on the table, and send text messages; a "jerk" who would speak sarcastically and say things like, "Are you kidding me?" and "Clearly, you've never taken a business class before"; or a "depressive pessimist" who would look like his cat had just died, complain that the task was impossible, express doubt that the team could succeed, and sometimes put his head down on the desk.

Felps's first finding was that even when other team members were exceptionally talented and intelligent, one team member's negative attitude brought down the effectiveness of the entire team. In dozens of trials conducted over monthlong periods, groups with one underperformer did worse than other teams by an alarming rate of 30 to 40 percent.

To make matters worse, the other members started mirroring the poor team member even in the short time frame of one class period. As Felps explains, "Eerily surprising was how the others on the team would start to take on his characteristics." When the impostor was a slacker, the rest of the group lost interest in the project. Eventually someone else would announce that the task just wasn't important. If the actor was a jerk, others in the group also started being jerks by insulting one another, speaking abrasively. When the actor was a depressed pessimist, the results were the starkest. Says Felps: "I remember watching this video of one of the groups. You start out all the members are sitting up straight, energized, and excited to take on this potentially challenging task. By the end they have their heads actually on the desk, sprawled out."[2]

> "If you spend most of your time coaching an employee up, trying to get them to 'get it,' you are hiring poorly."

A-Players Only Need Apply

You get what you pay for; hiring great people is an investment. Every employee is like a stock in your investment portfolio. The rock star rule is fewer employees paid more equates to a lower total labor cost. It has been said that one high performer delivers more than ten average employees in a creative environment. Not to mention, average employees bring down high performers. Performance is contagious.

Building a world-class culture is not only about finding high performers but removing poor ones. A great workplace to high performers is one in which they're surrounded by other high performers.

The Objective of a Company's Hiring Process

The objective of hiring is not simply to fill job openings with warm bodies. It doesn't matter if you are a small, medium, or large organization; or if you are the director of human resources, head of recruitment, or a department leader; or if you are hiring seasoned people with a certain level of expertise or less experienced people you will have to train. Regardless of all these factors, your number one job is to find a candidate who not only fits your culture but will enhance it. The first step is creating a world-class recruitment experience (RX).

A great leader and a great organization understand that just as much as the potential employee needs to be the right fit for their company and team, the company needs to be the right fit for the potential employee. If not, within the next six months, both the company and the person who was hired are likely to be back at the drawing board, with both parties looking for a new situation.

> "Great companies are great precisely because they stand for something special, different, distinctive. That means, almost by definition, that they are not for everybody."
> —Jeff Bezos

Creating a World-Class RX

Many companies hire poorly because they are casting their lines in the wrong ponds and getting wrong-fit applicants. The first step is branding your company as the employer of choice to prospective right-fit talent.

A great recruiting experience saves a company from costly mistakes such as wasted time, culture setbacks, weakened employee morale, under- or overtraining, employee turnover, and a negative impact on the customer experience.

Everything a brand does, internally and externally, must be an experience. As introduced in chapter 1, your organization needs to focus on being BX strong (brand eXperience strong), which is an entire experience ecosystem. The companies that will dominate their industries for the next decade will be the ones who are obsessed with evolving the experience at every level—employee, customer, vendor, and community.

We are not just talking about having a good or even great interview process that helps you better select the seemingly superior applicants. The problem with that is, who's to say the people who are applying are truly rock stars? And if they are rock stars, who's to say that they will accept your job offer? Today more than ever, rock star employees have plenty of choices.

Prior to the Great Resignation and labor shortage, if a person wanted a new job with a new company, they most likely would apply and interview with one company, then wait to hear if they got the job. Not today. People realize that the current landscape is an employee market. As a result, they are interviewing at several companies, looking for the best offer.

Now, "best offer" doesn't always mean highest compensation. It can mean many different things, typically a combination of factors including pay, opportunity for advancement, flexibility, workplace culture, hard and soft benefits, professional development, autonomy, mission, purpose, core values, meaning and purpose of the job they will be doing, and the type of leaders who will impact the person's development, personally and professionally.

Don't Show the Candidate What They Want; Show Them What They Can't Live Without

Now the challenge is, how can you articulate these facets in a recruitment experience? A person may think they know what is important to them from their past employment experiences, where they were probably just trading hours for dollars.

What you want to consistently have happen is: A candidate interviews with your company, then goes on interviews with different organizations, and those other businesses pale in comparison to your recruitment experience. The candidate actually becomes worried that they might not be selected by your company. That is what a world-class RX does for your brand.

RX Starts Long Before the First Interview

The branding of your culture needs to be strong and defined in every way a candidate can be exposed to—from what they see on your website, to your social media presence, to what existing and past employees have to say, to reviews on Glassdoor and other online employment sites, to customer reviews, to the interview process.

Everything potential employees see and hear should make overwhelmingly obvious what your brand stands for. Your company culture needs to be so definitively clear that one of two things happen: They are either turned on or turned off. And their being turned off is a great thing for both the company and the candidate. Neither the company nor the new employee needs to find out in three months that it wasn't a good match.

The number one way to increase a candidate's interest in working for your company is by educating them on how hard it is to get hired there. The top employee experience brands articulate that they are not for everyone, nor do they want to be. They are for the 2 percent who want to emerge as the best of the best, who are not afraid to work hard and challenge themselves to see how much greatness they have inside. Not only will potential candidates appreciate that, but it will also tell them that if they get hired, your screening process will protect their workplace culture, ensuring a "jerk-free" environment.

Don't Offer a Job, Offer a Career

From each employee candidate's first encounter with your brand to their first day of new employee orientation and throughout their career with your organization, make sure they are aware of the career opportunities that can result from their hard work and rock-star performance in helping the company grow. Share examples of your own rags-to-riches stories of people who started off at entry-level positions, many of whom probably thought they were in a temporary transitional job. However, because of the culture, they stayed and rose through the ranks, and their efforts and loyalty were rewarded. Today they are some of the top leaders in your company, who have had the biggest impact not only on the organization's success but on team members' lives.

Share Your Vision and Tie It to Your Employees' Jobs

Leaders need to be constantly reminded that human beings need meaning and purpose in their jobs. It shouldn't be a shock that so many employees don't stay in jobs that aren't engaging or inspiring them. Most people want more than competitive wages and health insurance; they want to be part of something bigger. Whether you are a recruiter or leader, during an employee's career, especially during the interview stage, you must help them see your vision of what their short-term and long-term future could look like with your company. When done right, your vision becomes their vision. That is a powerful transformation, a game changer for an employee to have someone who believes in them and what they are capable of.

Narrow Down Your Talent Pool

If you go to the career page on most companies' websites, they all tend to be saying the same generic messages. Every company has a mission and purpose statement. Every company has core values. No one reads those and says, "They value respect, so do I; I want to work for them." People don't believe what they read; they believe what they experience. One of Enron's core values was integrity: "We work with customers and prospects openly, honestly, and sincerely. When we say we will do something, we will do it; when we say we cannot or will not do something, then we won't do it."[3] Enron's core values were prominently displayed in their annual reports, its corporate code of ethics, and other company communications. However, the company's actual practices and behavior did not always align with these values, as evidenced by the financial scandals that ultimately led to Enron's collapse in 2001.

> "If every employee at your company had to reapply for his or her job annually, how many would you be rehiring?"
> —Donna Cutting, author

The absolute best recruiting and culture companies stand out and articulate their mission, purpose, and values with energy, clarity, and gusto. You clearly know what type of culture they have and whether you would be a fit or not. Take, for example, Atlassian, an Australian tech company. Atlassian does an incredible job showcasing their five core values in a video in a no-nonsense manner:

1. Open company, no BS

2. Build with heart and balance

3. Don't f*** the customer

4. Play as a team

5. Be the change you seek[4]

Atlassian is clearly not trying to appeal to everyone. Using explicit language to communicate their core values definitely will turn some potential candidates away. Thirty seconds into the video it is apparent what Atlassian is saying is, "We are not a traditional company. We are different and so are our people. Normal need not apply."

Atlassian brands itself on enabling their teams to develop remarkable products for their clients, while working in an environment where they feel valued for their skills and able to put ideas and innovations forward. "Culture is something that can't be manufactured. It's a combination of characters of all the people who live in the building," says Mike Cannon-Brookes, cofounder and co-CEO.[5]

Multiple Interviews

Getting hired at your company should be extremely hard. It is only fair to your existing employees that you stay exceptionally selective on whom you let in. People need to earn the right to be a part of your culture and legacy.

The best companies purposely don't make it easy to get hired. Unlike the many businesses that offer candidates a job before they have completed their applications, top brands make job candidates come in for three to four interviews over the course of several weeks. These companies also want to make sure that job candidates are not simply looking for the best deal when, on paper, they don't appear to be.

We have found the best interview process is:

1. Group interviews (multiple candidates at the same time)

2. One-on-one interview (potentially with multiple leaders)

3. Observation day

4. Job offer

Making Your Interview Process Ungameable

Many people are good at interviewing but are not good at their job. The biggest problem with the typical interview process is that most intelligent candidates can game it. Everyone knows they are going to get asked, "Tell me two negatives about yourself." A well-prepared candidate will respond, "I am a perfectionist and workaholic." The companies that hire the best have screening processes that are "ungameable." Oftentimes the questions we ask a candidate during the interview process are ones that stimulate conversations and get the candidate talking. You discover much more when you go down rabbit holes where the answers weren't rehearsed.

Interview like Lieutenant Columbo

Interviewing is extremely intimidating. When we interview someone, we consider it an anti-interview. We love to help get the candidates' guard down, get them relaxed and in conversation mode, forgetting all the prepared canned answers they have rehearsed.

We will start the interview with something like, "Lisa, before we get started, I see you graduated from Aurora High School. I know a lot of people from there. I hear great things about that school. Did you enjoy it? Did you know Mrs. Francis, who teaches Spanish?" This gets the candidate talking about her school, teachers, what activities she was involved in. It allows the interviewer to take the conversation down many rabbit holes.

Gold is in the rabbit holes. You can find out so much from jumping conversations and seeing patterns: Is this person genuinely happy, are they positive or negative, were they a victim, did they not play because the coach had favorites who weren't as good? While this entire conversation is happening, the potential employee subconsciously thinks the interview hasn't started yet. Obviously, from the moment they walk into the building, they are on stage; the interview has started. We call it the Columbo interview style.

Lieutenant Columbo, portrayed by Peter Falk in the 1970s TV show *Columbo*, employs a unique method of interrogation that has proven effective beyond the realm of law enforcement. His technique involves a two-step process: first, encouraging the subject to open up and speak freely, and second, seamlessly introducing the critical question into the conversation.

Get Them Talking

Columbo initiates his interactions with relaxed and broad questions, creating a comfortable atmosphere that encourages open communication. His unkempt appearance and meandering walk convey a sense of harmlessness, while his seemingly perplexed mannerisms when he speaks reinforce the perception of his incompetence, solidifying the initial impression that he poses no threat. Compared to other more intimidating police officers, his demeanor is amiable, offering a pleasant break. His trivial banter serves to further put people at ease, leading them to willingly participate in conversations that divert their attention, all while he subtly steers the discussion.

Slip In the Real Question

Once the individual is at ease and a strong rapport has been established, Columbo skillfully introduces a question pertaining to his actual area of interest. Another tactic he employs, particularly when the individual's guard is lowered, is to pose a final inquiry right as he is making his exit. At this point, the person being interrogated has mentally concluded the interaction and is anticipating the relief of solitude. Consequently, Columbo's unexpected question catches them by surprise, prompting an unguarded response as they aim to swiftly conclude the interaction.[6]

An article on motivational interviewing (MI) via the Australian Mental Health Academy describes the "Columbo approach" this way: "Proponents of motivational interviewing owe a debt of gratitude to the 1970s television series *Columbo* . . . [Columbo] was a master of the skill of 'deploying discrepancies,' and MI therapists/practitioners can use the same skill to get clients to help them make sense of their (the clients') discrepancies."[7]

British forensic psychologist and professor Ray Bull mentioned in an interview with the *Times* newspaper how British police use an "investigative interviewing technique. These interviews sound much more like a chat in a bar. It's a lot like the old

Columbo show, you know, where he pretends to be an idiot but he's gathered a lot of evidence."[8]

Group Interviews

In our own businesses, John Robert's Spa and The DiJulius Group, we have found group interviews to be extremely productive and telling. The first round of interviews is always with a group of candidates. This reduces the time from several hours spent meeting multiple candidates to a one-hour interview with several candidates. This initial interview starts with what the company is about, what the position is about, and what it takes to be successful at both. We then ask the candidates questions that each must take turns answering. The potential hires think they are being judged on who has the best answer, but what we are really observing is what the other candidates are doing when it is not their turn to answer. Are they disengaged or fidgety? Or are they listening, nodding, and smiling while the other person is answering the question? That is the one we want.

The Engagement Indicator—the Five Es

If you are seeking people who have the potential to be customer-centric team members, evaluating their five Es (see below) might be your most powerful tool. Many of our consulting clients have incorporated the five Es into their interview process, literally counting the times a candidate demonstrates each one. For example, they might record the number of times during the interview that:

- Eye contact is made
- Ear-to-ear smiles take place

- Enthusiasm is displayed

- Engagement with the interviewer occurs naturally

- Educated answers are given to interview questions

While we believe most employee candidates have the potential to provide excellent customer service, not all do. The five Es can help you identify candidates who are able to achieve a high service aptitude with rigorous training.

During the interview process, if candidates are not smiling, making eye contact, and showing enthusiasm, we pass. No amount of customer service training will change them. One word of caution: If the person conducting the interview is not consistently executing the five Es, you cannot expect candidates to be.

Observation Day

Companies that obsess about protecting their internal culture typically have a candidate come in for an observation day during the interview process, where they come and observe the team/department they are interviewing to join. They get to see what their role would look like in action and to interact with existing team members who are their potential future coworkers. We try to give information to the employee the candidate is shadowing, including the candidate's FORD—which stands for family, occupation, recreation, and dreams (which will be discussed in great detail in the following chapters)—so existing employees can personalize their observation experience and make the candidate feel more comfortable.

We like to educate the candidate that the observation day is for them to interview us: Check out our culture, what their potential future environment looks and feels like. Talk to as many existing employees as possible. Ask them anything. Stay as long as you wish. An employee candidate needs to leave that observation day being able to say one of two things: either this is the place for me, I loved their energy and how they worked together, or the opposite. Either answer is a victory for both parties.

Guardians of Your Culture

The observation day for potential employees also allows for many existing team members to meet the candidate and share input on whether they think this person would be a right fit. The more existing employees (not only leadership) are included, the more they take ownership of protecting their culture. The best part of this process is, when those candidates start working, the existing employees whom they met during the interview process go out of their way to help them feel welcomed and take ownership in their success.

Kissing Up versus Kicking Down

Kissing up versus kicking down is a term used to describe whether a person is polite and flattering only to those they feel can be key to their success and unfriendly or indifferent to those they think can't help them. That is why the observation day is so critical. Follow up with every employee who encounters the candidate, not just those on her interview schedule. How did she treat your parking lot attendant? Your receptionist? Your administrative assistant? Is the candidate kind, gracious, and respectful to everyone they interact with?

Undercover Interviewers

There are great stories of companies that have the person driving the candidate from the airport end up being the CEO to see how the candidate treats someone they perceive has no real value to them if they get hired.

Survivor

When interviewing for a job at Pret a Manger, a sandwich shop, potential new hires are asked to spend time at one of the store's locations.[9] Then existing employees at that location vote whether to hire or not. Ninety percent of prospects get a thumbs-up. Those who don't make the cut are sent away. The crucial factor is gaining support from existing employees. Those workers have skin in the game: Bonuses are awarded based on the performance of an entire team, not individuals. Pret workers know that a bad hire could cost them money.

What investment did they make?

One way or another, everyone you hire contributes to your culture. A big difference between finding future rock stars versus the posers is finding out what investment the candidate made to learn about your organization.

Jesse Cole is the founder of Fans First Entertainment, parent company of the Savannah Bananas, a world-famous baseball circus that travels around the country entertaining fans unlike any other baseball team ever has. Cole is the Walt Disney of sports entertainment. What he gets his employees and ballplayers to do is extraordinary. John has spoken to their organization and attended their games and been blown away by the experience.

Everyone who works there delivers, from parking lot attendants to ticket takers, food vendors to the players.

Working for the Savannah Bananas is not for everyone, probably not for the vast majority of the human population. Jesse's amazing culture is made up of what most leaders think are the most difficult workers to manage, millennials and Gen Zers.

So how does Jesse find the rare individual who can maintain the incredible reputation the Savannah Bananas has created and fans have come to expect? "For us, it all boils down to authenticity. We lead the entire recruitment/application process being genuine in who we are and what we stand for and allow space along the way for candidates to make the decision themselves if they'd like to be part of the organization," says Cole. "In fact, I'd argue that we more often try to 'scare' candidates away by sharing with them that our fast-paced and ever-changing environment isn't for everyone."

The Savannah Bananas has projects and assignments they ask candidates to complete after each phase of the interview process that aren't particularly challenging or time consuming. "The 'wrong' person fails to see the value in the project and will either submit a lackluster version or will self-eliminate entirely. The right candidates get even more fired up about the opportunity because those extra steps continue to show how different we are from other organizations," explains Cole.[10]

Cover Letter Videos and Future Resume Videos

Part of Jesse Cole's employee interview process is to have all the candidates submit two videos: a cover letter and a future resume. "Video cover letters are huge for us because we can immediately see personality and enthusiasm from a person. Do they lift us up? Do they bring energy?" Cole shares. "For us, both the video cover letter and future resume are tests on our core beliefs of the Fans First Way. These core beliefs are: Always Be Caring, Different, Enthusiastic, Fun, Growing, and Hungry. The 'Always Be' is important because if we don't see some of these traits from their first video introduction to us, we know it will be hard to get that out of them as a future employee."

In a video cover letter, Cole's team can spot enthusiasm and fun immediately. With a future resume, they can see traits like growth and hunger. Cole says, "What do they want to do in the next five years? Ten years? Do they want to be in the same position, or do they want to grow more and make a bigger difference?"

This also gives Cole's team an opportunity to see the candidates' creativity. How are they filming the video cover letter? What are they wearing? Where are they? Is it something normal or is it different? This is another one of their core values.

The future resume video also shows how the candidate aligns with Savannah Bananas' core values. How is the layout? What projects do they share that they will work on? How much fun do they have with it, or is it basic and boring? "Within a few seconds on the video, we can tell if we want to hang out with that person. All of our positions are outward facing, and we work with our fans regularly, so this is important. If we don't want to hang out with them, if they don't bring energy and lift us up, why would our fans want to be around them either?" says Cole.

"Once they've made it through the entire interview process, we bring them out to the stadium to make an official offer and to introduce them to the entire team. By this time, they are fully aware an offer will be extended in person, and if we've done our job right, they're ready to accept on the spot. Then we cue up the champagne toast," explains Cole.[11]

Don't Ask Them What "They" Would Do in a Situation

In his book *Give and Take: Why Helping Others Drives Our Success*, author Adam Grant suggests a great way to screen out the potential employee candidates who don't align with your organization's value. Grant suggests presenting them with situational interviews. But not the way most organizations do them.

"A lot of organizations do behavioral interviews that are backward looking and asking about your history, what you've accomplished, what challenges you've overcome, and those actually don't turn out to be very effective. They suffer from an apples and oranges problem, it's very hard to compare it to people's work histories," explains Grant.

Even taking it one step further, Grant doesn't suggest asking the candidate what they would do in a given situation, because most people would give the "right" answer, not necessarily how they would truly react in that situation. What Grant does suggest is, instead of asking, "What would you do?" ask "How do you think most people would handle . . . ?"

Grant explains that most of us tend to project our own motivations onto other people. So, if you give someone a scenario where it's not clear what the appropriate behavior is, people will tend to predict based on what they would do in that situation, not realizing they just shared some insight on what they likely would do in the same situation.[12]

The Wrong Order Test

A great way to test someone's character is to observe how they react when things don't go according to plan. Whenever Walt Bettinger, CEO of Charles Schwab, is involved in an interview, typically C level, he takes the candidate out for a breakfast interview. What the potential executive is not aware of is Bettinger has asked the restaurant to purposely mess up the candidate's order. As Bettinger sees it, character is everything, and the "wrong order" test is meant to gauge how a potential hire deals with adversity. "It's just another way to look inside their heart rather than their head," says Bettinger.[13]

Competency Can Be Taught; Character and Chemistry Cannot

Competency is a critical part of Chick-fil-A's recipe, yet it is not the number one priority in their selection process. Most companies start with competency. However, competency can be taught, and in many customer interacting positions you can find hundreds of employees with similar skill sets. Chick-fil-A chooses to prioritize character and chemistry over competency, and it begins with conversation.

During the interview process, Chick-fil-A likes to focus on asking questions such as "Why do you want to do this?" The what and the how are elementary, but the candidate's "why" is where authenticity is revealed. After the initial interview, Chick-fil-A takes the strategy even deeper, testing whether this person really wants to do this job, and even whether existing employees want the potential candidate to be their colleague. They use experiential interviews toward the end to put them in a restaurant and observe them, as well as giving them time to shadow existing employees, so the candidate can really see what this job is like and even more importantly, get a feel for if it is truly right for them. And vice versa.[14]

Hire for the Soul, Train for the Role

When great brands look for great employees, they place a higher value on their will versus their skill. If they have the will, they can teach them the skill. If you want happy employees, only hire happy people. Be picky; hold out for people who ooze enthusiasm and positivity. Negative people are like a virus that spreads quickly. Steve Jobs once said, "It is too easy, as a team grows, to put up with a few 'B' players, and they then attract a few more 'B' players, and soon you will even have some 'C' players. 'A' players like to work only with other 'A' players, which means you can't indulge 'B' players."[15]

Hiring new employees should not be your top priority. Instead, focus on creating an amazing internal culture with high morale and low turnover. High employee attention will produce high employee retention, which is much easier and less expensive than recruiting new employees. What happens when you hire amazing people is that they are disappointed when they must work with mediocre people. Every time you select someone, your culture gets better or worse.

Be careful where you are giving your attention, however. If you waste a lot of time with high-maintenance employees, you end up neglecting the quiet, unsung heroes who deserve your attention.

Where did all the workers go?

This is probably the most frequent question we have heard business leaders ask: Where have all the workers gone, and how can we attract and keep them? Nearly every industry is struggling with finding enough workers to run fully staffed. For so many, the pandemic was a professional awakening, causing many employees to reevaluate their professional careers, not only what they want but also what they're no longer willing to tolerate.

An overlooked segment of the labor pool is what we call

the "discretionary workforce." The discretionary workforce includes those groups who do not have to work; in the past, pre-pandemic, they chose to work. Who, specifically are the people falling into this category?

1. People around retirement age. Many people enjoy working and don't want to retire.

2. Recent college graduates who decide to delay starting their careers (stay on Mom and Dad's payroll) because graduate school with its further degree requirements looks like a better alternative.

3. Stay-at-home parents who don't need to work for financial reasons but like to work a few days a week for sanity purposes.

4. The "gig economy" is another crevasse in the labor pool, with hidden workers who continue to reduce the available workforce. They include those former employees who are looking for independence, for example, solopreneurs, Uber drivers, life coaches, virtual assistants, freelance artists, and other nontraditional workers.

Seize the Opportunities

While these four segments of our workforce were not a top priority in the past for most organizations, they are a tremendous opportunity for a talented labor pool, for the businesses that make themselves attractive to these groups.

According to the US Census Bureau, approximately 10,000 people in the United States turn 65 years old every day. These are members of the baby boomer generation, which refers to those born between 1946 and 1964. Organizations with inclusive company cultures leveraging this age group in their workforce will enjoy a competitive edge going forward, both from retaining a broad range of talent and enjoying a deeper understanding of their aging customer base.

Where did all the women go?

An article in *TIME* magazine talks about a disturbing trend that occurred during the height of the COVID-19 pandemic: 885,000 women left the workforce, while only 216,000 men exited during that same period.[16] And that's not all. In addition to these higher resignation rates, one in four women cut back on hours or changed their role to one that is less demanding. When fewer women are in the workforce, there's an increase in gender pay gaps and a lack of diversity in senior executive roles, and the lower number of women could potentially lead to some level of employee attrition. For the women who have remained in the workforce, however, this tight labor market can offer a time for development opportunities.

The impact of a discretionary workforce on the labor shortage has been extremely underestimated. It is also a great group to try to recruit into your job opportunities. Shifting from the Great Resignation by capitalizing on the Great Retention starts with attracting and keeping women and an older workforce.

"Women's labor force participation rate in the U.S. has been set back 33 years, and gender pay equity has been set back 23 years," says Jean Accius, former senior vice president of AARP, in an article from 2022. "There's very little gender equity in there. Childcare is important. Paid leave is important. But they are not silver bullets." For more inclusive workplaces tomorrow and beyond, there must be a commitment to equity as well as an overseeing of the commitment. If this can be achieved, Accius believes the positive impact on employee acquisition and retention, and the economic impact on companies and our economy in general will be tremendous.[17]

During volatile economic periods, many businesses mistakenly play defense instead of offense when it comes to hiring. However, if you have the capital and revenue, these volatile times are the best for hiring, because others aren't doing that. You will then find your company in a strong position when the economy returns.

We have had the pleasure of working with NewDay USA, a mortgage company for active service members, veterans, and their families, for nearly a decade now. NewDay's commitment to providing a world-class veteran experience is impressive to say the least. And like any organization that is committed to consistently delivering a world-class customer experience, the type of employee they attract and hire is critical.

The mortgage industry is extremely competitive when it comes to recruiting new employees from colleges. Franco Greco, innovative chief revenue officer at NewDay USA, shares how NewDay differentiates itself in the recruiting wars. "We follow a meticulously scripted recruiting process. Candidates are required to visit our office for a firsthand experience, which we fondly refer to as 'hitting the marble.' During their visit, candidates spend a minimum of an hour shadowing an Account Executive (AE) to deeply understand the role they're applying for. We maintain a professional aesthetic, requiring candidates to wear suits for their interviews, aligning with our in-house AE dress code. Interviews are conducted by potential mentors. Interestingly, these mentors must voluntarily offer their time for training, even if it means pausing their regular duties. This ensures that mentors are genuinely invested in their mentees' growth."[18]

NewDay USA

First Interview Script

Road to Marble Floor

Good [Morning/Afternoon/Evening] [Candidate Name], [Your Name] following up from NewDay USA. How are you?

Great, [Candidate Name]. The goal of this call is for you to learn about NewDay, and I want to learn a lot about you. For us to have a successful partnership, I want both of us to share the good, the bad, the ugly, and set proper expectations, because if either of us are surprised six months from now, we're both going to be hurt!

What makes us different?

I would like to start off expanding on what makes us different at NewDay, and at any point if you want to stop me to learn more and ask questions, please do. NewDay is an interesting blend of cutting edge tech and data science, but it's also an old-fashioned family business. We place an incredible focus on mathematics and information-driven analytics.

Our business was founded by our CEO in 1999 with $300,000 of his own cash in the small town of Columbia, Maryland. Over the past 25 years, NewDay has been built into a nationwide mortgage company licensed in 43 states, specializing in helping military families achieve their financial goals, with three offices in Maryland,

Indiana, and Florida. Our company has zero debt, zero funding from private equity and operates as a family business.

Where is the opportunity?

Now *[Candidate Name]*, you might ask, where is the opportunity? It's important to understand, we are a niche financial services provider, and we specialize in serving the underserved veteran community. While banks and other lenders are tightening their lending guidelines, NewDay uses our proprietary data-driven approach so we can say YES to those who have been told no by banks.

With the cost of everything going up, from food to gas, families are hurting. Over the past year, interest rates on credit cards have gone up, and car loan rates have increased as well! Many military families don't have a resource to help structure their finances and build them a plan to move forward.

When you look at who the financial advisor is in today's world for the middle class, it's no longer Merrill Lynch or UBS, but rather it's NewDay USA. As an Account Executive you are helping veteran families take advantage of record home equity to take cash out and save over $4000 per year by paying down their high interest rate debts.

Do you have any specific questions about NewDay in general that I could help answer?

What's your story?

Now I want to gain some more insight into your background, *[Candidate Name]*. Tell me a little bit about where you grew up. What kept you busy in high school?

What made you choose to go to school at *[College Name]*? How was your experience?

Work Experience

- What did you do outside of coursework during the school year?
- What did you do during the summers?
- What makes you want to get into sales?
- What sales experience do you have?
- What core values should every salesperson possess? *[NewDay has core values of Integrity and World-Class Service]*

Influences

- Where do you get your work ethic from?
- What is the best advice you've ever received?
- Who is someone you idolize?

Resilience

- Name a 90-day period of your life/career during which you were the hungriest to succeed? What drove you?
- Have you ever had a losing streak? How did you turn it around?
- What is the most difficult thing you had to overcome and how did you learn from it?
- How would you exceed expectations in this role?
- Now *[Candidate Name]*, I'd like for you to balance in your own mind, how do you deliver results while also being a team player?

Training

Have you taken any classes in marketing? Mortgages? Are you familiar with the industry?

Good thing is, we require no prior industry experience. We, in fact, prefer you do not have too much experience because we believe in training the next generation of mortgage bankers from the ground up. Your first month of employment you'll receive world-class training through the NewDay University, where we'll pay you to study and learn! You will be studying for the SAFE exam, which is something you need to pass to jargon. Week one will be lecture, week two is self-study, and that final week will be practice exams getting ready for the real thing!

Once you graduate from the University, we will license you in 14–15 states, which again, is completely paid for by NewDay. You will then start training camp where you will learn how to do the job, how to read credit reports, order appraisals, take applications, and learn our sales script. You will then start the apprentice program for on-the-job training. As an apprentice, you are assigned a one-on-one mentor who will sit next to you and show you how to be successful over the next ten weeks. On a daily basis, you will learn how to sell by shadowing their calls, learn how to build and manage a pipeline and understand credit risk, while also gaining key skills in business, management, and leadership.

Your mentor is a high producer and is compensated on your success, so they are going to make sure they do everything they possibly can to make sure that you WIN!

The Account Executive position is our client-facing sales career. We offer a starting salary of $60K, uncapped commissions, monthly, quarterly, and yearly bonus incentives, plus paid licensing, training, and leads. Once you're promoted to the sales floor, many of our AEs are on track to earn north of six figures by the end of year one on the phones. By year two, AEs have developed confidence and a full understanding of our sales process, putting them in a position to earn between $150 and $200K. In the third year, 66 percent of our team members are able to go out and purchase their own home!

Over the past ten years, we've invested over half a billion dollars into building the NewDay brand, and we drive pre-qualified inbound leads to our AEs' phones—so there's no "cold-calling." We invest about $70 million a year on advertising; $25 million is spent annually on our nationwide TV campaign on Fox News, which airs three times per hour. In addition to our TV campaign, we've had incredible success with our direct mail campaign, which uses data science and information-driven analytics to find veterans who 1.) need money, 2.) own homes, 3.) have equity, and 4.) have debt, which makes this one of our highest performing and desirable lead sources.

As an Account Executive, you are the only point of contact for the veteran from start to finish. How the process works is the veteran calls in, and you'll learn their unique story, what their goals are and what they are trying to accomplish. You'll complete a full application, where you'll talk about their home, income and credit, figure out how much debt they are in, and how much equity they have access to in their home. You're educating them on how they can use their VA home loan benefit to save money and plan for retirement. A significant amount of veterans in the US do not take advantage of their VA benefits . . .

Ultimately, [Candidate Name], this role is highly lucrative but more so, it is fulfilling. This role has more of an advisory approach, working directly with the veteran and their family throughout their entire process. Your goal is to create a financial plan that they qualify for and build a strong relationship with the military families you serve and put them in a better financial place than they are in now.

Culture

When seeking a new job, how important is culture in your decision? What is your current culture like? How old are most of your colleagues? Do you connect with them pretty well?

What I enjoy most about NewDay is the people, and it's not like your typical corporate job, especially in the banking world, where the average age is 45–50 years old. Our company average is closer to 26 years old. With younger employees we are fast-paced, energetic, and filled with ambitious, competitive, and like-minded professionals, usually earlier in their careers. With our open floor plan and NFL-style team-based culture it is easy to build long lasting friendships. We really push each other to get 1 percent better each day and are very competitive with one another!

NewDay hosts a ton of company events to create a family-like environment. We celebrate our success with steak and beans competitions, tequila parties and company happy hours, box seats and tickets to Dolphins games. We host a bunch of team and departmental competitions.

We definitely like to work hard and play hard!

Growth

Are you someone who is interested in future leadership opportunities or a managerial position?

NewDay promotes from within. All our senior management and the majority of our C-suite started at the base level (CA or AE) like you and worked their way to the top through our Executive Management Leadership Program! There is no ceiling on where you can go at NewDay USA, and it's a true meritocracy.

At NewDay, we provide exciting opportunities and rewards for our high-performing Account Executives. Our AEs have the chance

88   The Employee Experience Revolution

to aim for the prestigious President's Club, where the top ten performers can enjoy the flexibility of working remotely for a few days a week. In addition to this, President's Club recipients are also honored with the SOUL award, which includes all-inclusive trips to luxurious Four Seasons resorts in various locations.

For those looking to accelerate their career growth, our Executive Management Leadership Program offers invaluable benefits. Participants in this program receive personalized one-on-one mentorship from our C-level executives, engage in leadership development from CEO coach Sheldon Harris, and experience world-class customer service training guided by John DiJulius.

Recognizing that high performers may have different goals, we also offer an alternative path called the Admiral's Club. This pathway is designed for individuals who excel in producing results. Once you become a member of the Admiral's Club, you'll gain access to exclusive benefits such as a hybrid work schedule, opportunities to attend prestigious events like the World Series, team trips to scenic Kiawah Island, and even Miami Dolphins suite tickets.

At NewDay, we believe in providing diverse and rewarding paths for our talented individuals, empowering them to achieve their professional aspirations.

Good, Bad, Ugly

Lastly, *[Candidate Name]*, we have a culture of excellence here at NewDay and should we decide to move forward together, I want to set proper expectations by breaking out the good, the bad, and the ugly.

- Good
  - Market to veterans w/ debt and equity
    - No cold calling

- ○ Life changing $
- Bad
    - ○ It's a sales job, and we're going to invest $360,000/year into making you successful by providing you leads, sales training, leadership development, and licensing. We ask in return that you produce, and the reality is not everyone is successful, even with the constant training.
    - ○ We have a defined sales process that has been refined by top performers and mortgage executives over the past 25 years.
        - » 20-page sales script
            - * Willing to follow
        - » Sales psychology
            - * Ask questions to veteran
- Ugly
    - ○ Work: 49 hours
        - » 1.5 Saturdays / month (10 a.m.–3 p.m.)
    - ○ In office
        - » You're not working in your parents' basement in your pajamas; we come into work every day to serve veteran families and grow in our careers.

The Close

Do you have any questions before I speak on next steps?

Great, on a scale from 1–10 how prepared are you to move forward with this opportunity?

[If score 8 or below: Read below, then proceed to "this is my direct number"]

[Candidate Name], I appreciate you sharing. Based on our conversation you have a lot to think about . . . Please send me an email tomorrow morning before noon if this is something you want to pursue further.

[If score 9 or 10]

Excellent, the next step would be to invite you to our Career Day. We select candidates from across the country to join us for a half day in the office for a tour, a presentation by our VP of Credit Risk, Jae-han Kim, introductions to C-Level executives, a shadowing session for the role to learn more about the day to day, and finally interviews to see if you are a good fit for us. This is a great opportunity for you to showcase yourself in front of leadership and other candidates.

[In FL]: We have Monday the [date] or Wednesday the [date] available for you to join us at our new corporate headquarters at 360 Rosemary. What date would be best for you?

Great! I will send over a confirmation email with a calendar invite laying out details of the interview, what to expect. We are extremely selective in who we trust with our veterans and would like for you to spend time providing thoughtful answers to a few questions I'll send your way.

[Candidate Name], this is my direct number. Feel free to save my contact. It was great talking with you today, *[Candidate Name]*. Have a nice rest of your day and I will talk with you again [date/time scheduled]. Bye.

5

CREATING AN EMPLOYEE ONBOARDING EXPERIENCE

"As leaders we are in the human development business."

Picture this: You are excited to be starting a new career at a company that seems so promising. Your new career is about to start today, your first day of work. Few things in life are as exciting (and nerve wracking) as starting a new job. However, your first few days are consumed with reviewing policies and procedures from an employee handbook, which should really be called the "How not to get fired" handbook.

Onboarding should be about how to have an incredible career at an incredible company—a celebration of a great employee joining a remarkable culture that together will do incredible things. According to Gallup, 88 percent of employees are disappointed in their new organization's onboarding,[1] which leads to what Joey Coleman refers to as "hire's remorse" in his book *Never Lose an Employee Again*.

The Employee Experience Is Won and Lost in the Transitions

When dealing with a customer or an employee, the transition (aka handoff) from one department to another is critical—for example when a new employee goes from the interview process to orientation to the first week starting in their new department. All these transitions and handoffs influence how the new employee is made to feel. Too often when an employee starts their first day on the job, their supervisor isn't expecting them. No one has told the boss that a new employee is starting today. The new team member arrives thrilled to change the world. However, the supervisor is caught off guard, unprepared. Nothing is set up and ready to go, from equipment, supplies, to how the employee will be trained. The boss can be noticeably annoyed due to the unexpected inconvenience. How does that make the new team member feel? They start questioning their decision to take this job. They start thinking that the HR person overpromised and painted an unrealistic rosy picture of what it is like to work here.

> **"When I hire someone, that is when I go to work for them."**

Start Onboarding Before the New Hire Begins

Transitions are key. Whenever an employee is handed over to a new team or department, a warm handoff and onboarding is key. To ensure a smooth transition for your new hire and their team, start the new team member onboarding process at least a week before your new hire's start date. Work with the IT department and any other relevant personnel to make sure the new employee has a fully functioning workstation along with the login credentials to any systems or software they'll need to perform their job. This will make for a seamless first day and a positive first impression.

In his book *Never Lose an Employee Again*, author Joey Coleman emphasizes the critical job offer/acceptance stage that often gets overlooked. John had an aha moment when he realized his businesses tended to suck at this. "Basically, we tell them they got the job, when their start date is, and we will see them then."

Coleman calls this the Accept phase. "The Accept phase offers the chance to capitalize on the euphoria associated with this offer and acceptance, while creating a memorable moment at the instant the candidate becomes an employee. When a candidate accepts your job offer, you must show them how excited you are and make them feel wanted. Many organizations fail to see the opportunity to create a milestone memory in the actual extending of the job offer: a feeling of being wanted . . . stop and consider the times in your life when someone let you know they wanted you."

This is where it gets really interesting. Coleman shares, "When a prospective employee decides to accept your job offer, a physiological reaction takes place in their body. Brain science shows that when a prospective employee moves from a state of consideration to a decision to accept an offer, a chemical is released in the brain. Dopamine floods the gray matter, creating an emotional euphoria. The newly minted employee feels excitement and joy because their job search is over. They believe they have found what they were looking for all along. In this euphoric state, an employee is filled with hope for their future. They anticipate continued growth and learning, the chance to contribute to a larger cause or mission, possibilities of advancement, new challenges, and exciting opportunities. They plan to meet new people, do new things, be exposed to new situations, and achieve new things.

"At this key moment in the relationship—when both parties are thrilled that the search is over, and a decision has been made—the employer and employee often communicate asynchronously. An email or letter is sent, a decision is made, and an email or letter is sent back. Asynchronous interactions usually don't feel celebratory, and such an important occasion deserves to be celebrated. Don't miss the chance to capitalize on your new employee's excitement—and join them in the jubilation!" says Coleman. He concludes, "Magnifying the excitement and enthusiasm around a new employee joining your team gives them a boost of confidence that they made the right decision. Promoting their commitment to your organization publicly celebrates the new hire and builds broader interest in your enterprise. Using social media platforms to creatively announce new team members highlights your ongoing hiring efforts and praises your new team member in the same message."[2]

Send a Before-the-Start-Date Email

Author and professor David Burkus shares several tips on how to create some special moments even before a new employee starts.

"The first tactic to make new employees feel welcome is a before-the-start-date teaser email. You've been interacting [with] new hires during the interview process, and you know their contact information and you know a lot about them. So, before their first day on the job, preferably just a day or two before their start date, send them a quick email sharing how excited you are for them to join the team. Mention specific information you recall from the interviews and connect it to the work your team will be doing. Just that simple message can help them focus on what they're looking forward to and help them feel cared for and understood even before you're technically their team leader."[3]

The "Enter-view"

Burkus continues, "The second tactic to make new employees feel welcome is an 'enter-view.' This is sort of the opposite of the interview process. Instead of the new hires telling the team about themselves, it involves the team telling the new hires how excited they are to welcome them. Ideally members of the team were involved in the hiring process, and this enter-view is the chance for them to draw from what they remember to share why they're so excited for their new teammate. Enter-views work best when done in person early on the first day, but it could also be done by bombarding new hires' desks or email inboxes with positive messages throughout the day as well."[4]

Give a Personalized Welcome Gift

Find out about the new employee's FORD (family, occupation, recreation, and dreams). Burkus recommends, "Another tactic to make new employees feel welcome is to personalize their welcome gift. And personalization doesn't just mean adding their name to the card or even embroidering their name on a polo. Instead, it means welcoming them with a gift that is personally selected to appeal to them based on your knowledge about them. Then, when they arrive for their first day, that simple, personal gift is waiting for them."[5] The new employee's FORD offers ideas for directions to go on the personalized gift.

Orientation Is Critical

A critical part of a new employee's career is their orientation into the company. Psychologists have shown that during periods of orientation, people are particularly susceptible to adopting new roles, goals, and values.

Your new employee orientation training should not be about policy, procedures, and how not to get fired; rather it should be an emotionally compelling orientation into the company's values, mission, purpose, and storytelling. Tell the new employee about the company's backstory and early days, why the organization was created, what wrong was being made right. Include the company's struggles, how it overcame them, the rags-to-riches stories of today's rock star employees who started years ago at entry-level positions. Tell where the company is today and the amazing place it is headed (vision of the future). Most importantly, communicate the vital role new employees can play in helping the company achieve that vision and what is in it for them.

Most new employees are overwhelmed with the information overload and the insecurities of being a novice; they cannot fathom being a rock star someday. Hearing about someone who struggled early on and went on to great success can be inspiring to a new employee early in their career.

Your company's purpose and values don't truly come to life unless teams talk about them regularly in a structured way, and the best process involves team members telling their own stories about how a specific value or pillar impacted them personally.

"Most people come to work for a company having had previous work experiences. In many cases, their experience has been bad. As such, they enter with cynicism, and the burden of proof is on leaders to demonstrate that this is a different place."
—Howard Schultz, former CEO of Starbucks

Re-orientation

John learned a great lesson from consulting with The Ritz-Carlton Hotels—they put all their existing employees through the orientation process again. John immediately brought this idea back to his companies, and we instituted a re-orientation for all our existing employees every other year, meaning if you were hired in 2024, you would retake our orientation training in 2026, 2028, and so on.

Mixing experienced employees with new hires has had so many incredible benefits we didn't even anticipate. During key points in the orientation, experienced team members share great testimonials, telling stories of what it was like when they joined the company and what it was like back in the day. This immediately creates a bond between new and seasoned employees, which results in new employees having friends at work, and reducing the typical anxiety of being a new employee.

Most of all, re-orientation reinvigorates our seasoned staff. Many experienced employees have expressed great surprise at how much the orientation has improved and how much of our legacy they had forgotten about. They are reinspired by our story—where we came from, what it took to get us here, and where we are headed.

Scavenger Hunt

Most new employee orientations spend a great deal of time covering all the boring policy and procedures of how to avoid getting fired. While some of this information needs to be covered, Nemacolin Woodlands Resort, a Five Diamond property in Pennsylvania and a longtime client of The DiJulius Group, has a clever way to instill that information instead of sitting in a classroom. We have learned many techniques from working with Nemacolin; one of our favorites is the scavenger hunt they have their new associates experience. It is a competitive scavenger hunt on this huge resort where each new associate has a list of 50 things they must discover, find the answers to, and take pictures of. During the scavenger hunt, we realized two things: It is a lot of fun, and the new associates learn a lot about the history of Nemacolin. What a great idea!

Anytime we hear a great idea, we try to replicate it within our organization. Our organizations' orientation now includes a scavenger hunt across all our locations. We take a group of new employees, typically eight to twelve in a group, pair them up, give them a list of about 25 things to discover or get the answers to, and have them get pictures of every item on the list. This achieves many goals: The new employees have a great deal of fun; they work with another team member; they learn a lot about our culture, legacy, and heroes; and they visit multiple locations and meet many existing employees who go out of their way to help the new employees get their answers and pictures.

Sound Bite for New Employees

New employees are excited about their new opportunities, and during their first three months that is all they are talking about to their families, friends, and anyone they come in contact with. That is why, during orientation, it is critical that you give them a short sound bite to better articulate the specifics of their new job and the company they work for. For example:

> I just started working at The DiJulius Group as a customer experience consultant. The DiJulius Group is one of the top customer experience consulting companies, working with companies like The Ritz-Carlton, Lexus, Starbucks, KeyBank, Nestlé, Chick-fil-A, and

many more. We help organizations become the brand customers can't live without and make price irrelevant.

This sound bite gets them even more excited about their new career and is a great advertisement for potential employees and customers. It also sparks questions from the people they are talking to. We want their family and friends to say, "Wow, I want a job like that."

The First 90 Days Are Vital to an Employee's Career

For new team members, their first 90 days will leave a lasting impression and will dictate so much about their level of satisfaction with the choice they made for employment. Many organizations experience a significant percent of their turnover during the first 90 days of employment. According to an Indeed survey, 39 percent of employees who left a job within the first few months said more effective onboarding and training would have helped them stay longer.[6]

Why such high turnover during the first 90 days? For several reasons, the reality doesn't match the picture that was painted during the interview process and/or during orientation. Every single employee, when they start at a new company, knows the least of anyone. It is like being a freshman in high school all over again. However, in business, you typically don't have dozens and dozens of other people who are starting with you at the same time. Being the least knowledgeable person and a total stranger is not a pleasant feeling.

When you hire a new employee, the first three months is critical for establishing an emotional connection and loyalty to your brand. Implement a structured 90-day plan so you have a consistent process that makes new hires feel welcome, proud, and part of a championship team. Break down their first 90 days into a few key milestones to give and get feedback.

You Don't Grow Companies; You Grow People

Creating a positive and warm environment from the very first day establishes a world-class company culture for your new employee.

DAY 1 (OUTSIDE OF ORIENTATION)

1. Display a large banner in the employee lounge with the new team member's picture, name, and position.

2. Send a company-wide message in your internal communication channels introducing the newest team member, including their picture, title, and fun facts about their FORD.

3. Ensure all their paperwork is complete. If possible, send any forms that the employee needs to complete before their start date so they can hit the ground running on their first day. Otherwise, finishing paperwork should be the first item your new hire completes when they arrive.

4. Introduce them to their team members. Explain what each team member does and who will train and supervise them.

5. Educate them on who they need to go to for what—HR, payroll, their immediate supervisor, and so on.

6. Show them around the building. Introduce them to any departments they may work closely with, and show them key areas.

7. They should receive a detailed training schedule with dates, objectives, and who their trainer will be for each.

8. Assign a mentor who can offer guidance and answer questions. Their mentor should be a team member with seniority who possesses all the values you want your new employees to model.

9. Introduce all new employees at company meetings.

The JAM Session

In the book *Never Lose an Employee Again*, author Joey Coleman features a great example of how a company makes new hires feel welcomed on their first day. JAM Sports is based in Toronto and operates in more than a dozen cities across Canada and the United States. JAM connects people through play with their adult recreational sports leagues. In 27 years, JAM has grown significantly to a team of 400 employees.

"Built on a foundation of play and entertainment, JAM brings that same energy to their new-hire onboarding. On their first day at work, employees experience the High-Five Welcome. New hires are asked to show up at ten a.m. (an hour after the usual start time) so veteran employees can arrive at the office before the new team member," shares Coleman. "The director of HR keeps the entire team updated via their internal chat tool, while the new employee's team leader waits outside the building to welcome them upon arrival. The team leader ushers the new employee into the building, and they hear their walk-up song blaring from in-house speakers. Yes, you read that correctly. As part of the application process, the candidate is asked what their baseball 'walk-up' song would be, which JAM then uses to create an auditory experience (and memory) when they enter the building for their first day on the job. The new hire is greeted by a human high-five tunnel with veteran employees enthusiastically welcoming the newest member of the team."[7]

15-Day Check-In

The first two to three weeks can be the hardest for new team members. Being the new kid on the block usually comes with some bumps and bruises. You want to help pick up new employees if they need it. Do a check-in to learn how your new employee feels about their new job. This is also the time to share feedback and coach them on how they are performing, their attitude, and their progress. This is a great time to have them do a survey reviewing how their interview and orientation training was and how it could be improved for future hires.

30-, 60-, and 90-Day Check-Ins

Review the new hire's performance, feedback from their team members and mentor, and measurable key performance indicators (KPIs) if they apply yet. Use your core values as a measurement to how they are performing. Ask for their feedback. How are they feeling about their position and the support they are receiving? What could the company be doing better to set them up for success? This is the time to have them do an onboarding and training survey to help improve going forward. Ask the employee to begin thinking about some short-term goals they may want to achieve in the next 90 days. You and their mentor should be able to make suggestions for possible milestones they can meet. Document and provide specific, actionable feedback.

The first 90 days are crucial for employee retention. When you implement an onboarding program that makes new employees feel like they are welcomed, you're more likely to reduce turnover and increase loyalty. By checking in with your employee regularly and assigning a mentor, you'll build a stronger connection long term.

Buddy Program

Verbit, an AI company based in New York, has a fantastic way to build an emotional connection with new hires and seasoned employees. "To make it easier for our new employees, we established the 'Verbit Buddy Program,'" Renana Schamroth, the company's former vice president of HR, says in a *CTech* article from 2021. "This program entails a 'veteran' buddy being assigned to each new team member for their first three months on the job."

"The program is a win-win for both current and new employees. The new employee benefits are one-on-one assistance, a jump-start on networking, a single point-of-contact, knowledge of 'how things really get done,' and a smoother acclimation and onboarding process," Schamroth explains.[8]

Powerful First Impression

Growth guru Verne Harnish shares a great story in a LinkedIn post about how Redirect Health, a technology company based in Scottsdale, Arizona, has an excellent way of learning, capitalizing, and demonstrating FORD with their new employees. During the process of one-on-one interviews, the recruiting team asks the applicant, "What is an indulgence you love that is under $20?" They can see the culture and friendliness of the person in how they answer.

COO Guy Berry explains, "If we choose to hire a candidate, we have the item bought and waiting for the person when they show up on day 1. If we have a bunch of new team members, this creates great intro conversations as team members share what item they received. We have bought someone a specific or unique drink from Starbucks; special chocolates; pizza from specific restaurants for lunch; or even crazy socks that someone told us they love." It is a powerful first impression for the new team member and under $20!⁹

NewDay USA Onboarding Experience

Another great best practice by NewDay USA is their onboarding experience. "Our onboarding kick-starts with two engaging days termed 'JumpStart,' which educates new employees on all that NewDay has to offer; fun and team-building activities that create a camaraderie from day one. A group workout session and a *Shark Tank* presentation to senior managers on the second day," shares Franco Greco, a senior executive.

"Throughout the first month, our managers narrate their personal stories, offering inspiration and a sense of company culture. Our primary focus during this period is on a study test. However, our goal is to make this experience less academic and more of an exhilarating production, ensuring new hires remain enthusiastic about their journey with NewDay USA," explains Greco. "A cornerstone of our onboarding process is the Leadership Career Track. This track is instrumental in offering our new hires a clear path to strive for. Catering to the aspirations of Gen Z and millennials, we introduce them to growth trajectories and motivate them with the ethos: 'Work at NewDay not for what you can gain, but for who you can become.' This is why we have different leaders address them daily, sharing their transformative journeys."¹⁰

WHAT IS JUMPSTART?

- Career Kickoff
- Look into ND Culture
- Highlight Important Keys to Success
- Meet Key Leadership
- SOI!

NewDay USA

NewDay USA Account Executive Leadership Track

VICE PRESIDENT (3+ YEARS) $$$$$

- Opportunity to manage 50+ account executives, participate in business development functions, and receive exclusive trainings in business management from C-suite

ASSISTANT VICE PRESIDENT (2+ YEARS) $$$$

- Entrepreneurial opportunity with responsibility to hire, train, and motivate a team of account executives

AVP IN TRAINING (18–24 MONTHS) $$$

- Learn to manage high production team of 8–12 account executives while balancing high personal production

CAPTAIN (12–18 MONTHS) $$$

- Learn to manage a small team while producing at a high level
- Manage 2–4 account executives on your team

ACCOUNT EXECUTIVE (6–12 MONTHS) $$

- Certified Mortgage Professional
- Manage full sales cycle of personal pipeline

APPRENTICE (6 MONTHS) $$

- Learn mortgage business from top performers
- Mirror success habits

NewDay USA's Year Accelerated Underwriting Leadership Track

LEADERSHIP AND BEYOND $$$$$

- Opportunity to gain pure leadership experience in different operational positions, mentorship of others, responsibility for performance of team
- > 24 months

VA UNDERWRITER $$$$

- Evaluating risk and ability to repay, making loan decisions
- Opportunity to apply for VA designation and mentoring junior underwriters
- > 24 months

JR. UNDERWRITER $$$

- Underwriting live files, learning to evaluate risk and establish ability to repay, undergoing second review from senior underwriting manager
- Advanced MBA courses and final exam for CRU
- 10–18 months

CREDIT ANALYST $$

- Learning the basics of veteran loan eligibility, how to verify income and expenses
- Intermediate MBA courses
- 8–10 months

CLOSING AND FUNDING SPECIALIST $$

- Learn the closing and funding processes, ensure loans disburse correctly and mortgages are recorded legally
- Introductory MBA courses and the first exam
- 1–8 months

NewDay's Training Process

Every newcomer undergoes military training with the NewDay 5—a group comprising some of the most elite military personnel from the early 2000s. This training, termed "Veteran Military Orientation" (VMO), offers a profound understanding of the challenges faced by the veteran community, better educating a mostly nonveteran workforce. "Such exposure provides our employees with a purpose that transcends typical job roles, fostering a strong bond with our mission to assist veterans in dire need," NewDay's CEO, Rob Posner, explains.[11]

Franco Greco shares, "In essence, what sets NewDay USA apart, especially for millennials and Gen Z, is our dual focus: A clear progression plan that caters to their career aspirations and a noble cause that adds purpose to their profession. While compensation is undoubtedly essential, I firmly believe that these younger generations prioritize growth opportunities and impactful roles over mere financial gains."[12]

6

CREATING AN EMPLOYEE EXPERIENCE
THAT RETAINS THEM

"A great leader's goal should be that every long-term employee considers their decision to join this company as one of the best decisions of their life."
—JOHN DIJULIUS III

This chapter is all about building a moat around your talented employees. Let's revisit the definition of the Employee Experience Revolution:

> Great companies help people live extraordinary lives. Their leaders inspire employees to build lives of meaning and purpose.

One of the things John is proudest of as an entrepreneur is The DiJulius Group's leadership mission statement to our team members:

> We want you to make more money than you have thought possible. However, we want you to feel the money you made was the least valuable thing you received from this company.

John is proud of the mission statement, and of how we hold ourselves accountable to it. This is something we advertise to our employees constantly to make sure we are living up to it.

The first part of our leadership mission, "We want you to make more money than you have thought possible," is obviously measurable. It is the second part that we must define as leaders: "We want you to feel the money you made was the least valuable thing you received from this company."

The question is how do we become not only the best professional decision our employees have ever made, but one of the best decisions they ever made in their entire life, personally and professionally?

Forget Talent Wars; Grow Your Own Talent

It is vital that you make sure your employees are always learning and evolving in their craft, from internal classes to outside education (conferences and online learning) to consuming books, videos, and podcasts. Today it has never been easier to increase one's intellectual capital. One best practice we have learned is that whenever we send two or more team members to attend an education event, they are required to present to the rest of the team within ten days what they learned and how it applies to our organization.

Constant Professional Development

Too often the majority of an employee's training happens in their first few years with an organization. According to LinkedIn's Workforce Learning Report, 94 percent of employees say that they would stay at a company longer if it simply invested in helping them learn.[1]

> **"Once you stop learning, you stop excelling."**
> **—Reed Hastings, cofounder of Netflix**

This interest in learning and development is particularly strong among younger workers. LinkedIn's research found that roughly a quarter of Gen Zers and millennials say learning is the number one thing that makes them happy at work, and over a quarter (27 percent) of Gen Zers and millennials say the number one reason they'd leave their job is because they did not have the opportunity to learn and grow.[2]

> **"Employees will invest more of their heart and soul if they feel invested in."**

Great brands have employee evangelists of two things: what they do and who they do it for. When you do business with a world-class brand, you see a strong similarity; their employees love the industry they are in, love helping customers improve their lives with their product or service, and they love the brand they work for.

Recognize, Recognize, and Then Recognize Some More

Did you know that 63 percent of employees who are recognized regularly said they wouldn't consider looking for a new job?[3]

Our loved ones and coworkers are not telepathic about our appreciation; you have to be continually expressing your gratitude and appreciation.

> **"Feeling gratitude and not expressing it is like wrapping a present and not giving it."**

Employees Would Rather Be Criticized Than Ignored

According to a Gallup poll on the "State of the American Workplace," when bosses completely ignore employees, 40 percent of staffers actively disengage from their work. When the boss criticizes on a regular basis, 22 percent of employees actively disengage. So even if employees are being criticized, they are more engaged; they feel that at least someone is acknowledging that they exist! And if bosses recognize just a single strength and reward employees for doing what they're good at, only 1 percent actively disengage from the work they are expected to do. Added to those statistics is the fact that people who go to work unhappily do things, actively or passively, to make those around them unhappy, too.[4]

> **"We don't hire people with more winning qualities than anyone else. We just bring out their winning qualities."**

Never Forget About the Unsung Heroes

Recognize everyone, regardless of their position or title; ask for their input and opinions. You may be surprised by what you learn. When the CEO of the Charles Schwab Corporation, Walt Bettinger, was asked about the best lesson he learned in college, he answered that he wanted to graduate with a perfect 4.0 GPA, and it came down to his last final exam. "I had spent many hours studying and memorizing formulas to do calculations for the case studies. The teacher handed out the final exam, and it was on one piece of blank paper," explained Bettinger. "The professor said, 'I've taught you everything I can teach you about business in the last ten weeks, but the most important message, the most important question, is this: What's the name of the lady who cleans this building?'"

That test and lesson had a lasting impact on Bettinger. "It was the only test I ever failed, and I got the B I deserved. Her name was Dottie, and I didn't know Dottie." Although he had seen her many times, he'd never had a conversation with her, even if just to introduce himself and learn her name. "I've tried to know every Dottie I've worked with ever since. It was just a great reminder of what really matters in life, and that you should never lose sight of people who do the real work."[5]

Great Leaders Are Obsessively Grateful and Positive

Being shown appreciation for the work they do makes employees feel valued and proud. Celebrating small achievements helps people face larger challenges. It builds momentum. The experience of celebrating small accomplishments sets up a positive dynamic where everyone wants to do better. Routinely, frequently, and generously thanking team members costs nothing and has enormous benefits.

> **"A person will never go any higher than they think they can."**

Paying more, by itself, is not a long-term solution for retaining top talent. The most powerful approach to being proactive about talent is to invest in your existing team members. People have an insatiable need for attention. We all want to be seen, heard, and valued for our own unique set of skills and contributions. Data shows over and over that employees who receive weekly light-touch attention from their managers are three times more likely to be all-in at work.[6]

Be On a Mission to Catch People Doing Something Right

Do you have a system that reminds and inspires leaders to encourage others on a consistent basis? One of the most effective tools in boosting morale is our "Caught You Doing Something Right" card, which acknowledges some specific positive action or behavior a team member has executed. We keep stacks of these cards in the employee break room, call center, and any other room a team member enters. We started using them as a management tool, and now everyone has access to them. An employee may open his office drawer and find a "Caught You Doing Something Right" card thanking him for helping someone through a mini crisis the day before. Most employees collect and save these cards.

Our management team is required to catch people doing things right on a regular basis. This is so embedded in our culture that we now have a spreadsheet with every employee's name down one side and each manager's name across the top. The manager fills in the date they last sent each employee a "Caught You Doing Something Right" card. This way we can spot when someone hasn't been recognized in a while and immediately "catch" them.

We have even held "Caught You Doing Something Right" contests, and the employee who gives the most cards wins a gift certificate to a nice restaurant. The entire team really gets into it. One shy employee went home one night and wrote out over 100 personalized cards to everyone on our staff.

> **"The only time you should blame others for your results is when you are successful."**

Relationship Hacks

Numerous little investments in relationships are key to building that emotional connection. John learned a great relationship hack from reading Adrienne Bankert's book about kindness, *Your Hidden Superpower*. Bankert talks about the power of taking a few minutes to video message people instead of just texting them. So, John tried it, and to his amazement it was fast, easy, and the responses he got were incredible.

John has always texted his employees on their company anniversary dates and professional and personal milestones to thank and/or congratulate them. Now instead he sends a video message, which takes less time than typing and has a significantly bigger impact. Now John tries to force himself to think before he texts anyone—employees, clients, his sons—would this be more powerful as a video message?

Carpe Momento

The number one employee experience leaders can provide is a positive interaction with every team member they encounter.

You must create an emotional connection that's so engaging and compelling that the employee literally "feels" something afterward.

Carpe Momento—Seize the Moment: Our focus must be on providing a positive experience on every interaction.

How to Get Employees to Brag About Their Job

Think for a minute how much you talk about your time at work—with coworkers and clients, at home, on the golf course, out socially, even with strangers. For most people, work represents 25 to 50 percent of their total conversations.

As leaders, we need to give our employees something positive to talk about. Former CEO and current chairman of Gallup, Jim Clifton, shares the number one way you can change your culture immediately: "Have one meaningful conversation per week with each individual team member. It can be in person, email, over the phone. It can be for thirty minutes; it can be for five. Talk to them about their goals, obstacles/barriers; at the end of the day everyone is trying to win. Have it be about business."[7]

> "Imagine a world where people wake up every day inspired to go to work, feel safe while they are there, and return home at the end of the day feeling fulfilled by the work they do, feeling that they have contributed to something greater than themselves. Fulfillment is not a lottery. It is not a feeling reserved for a lucky few who get to say, 'I love what I do.'"
> —Simon Sinek

Knowing Your Employees' FORD

Leaders who have a relationship with their team will find that their employees are so much more engaged and bought in. When we help companies work on creating a world-class internal culture and better leadership skills, we always do an internal FORD (family, occupation, recreation, and dreams) exercise with the leadership team. We give them a list of the employees who report directly to them and see how much FORD they know. For example, do they remember the spouses' names, the spouses' occupations, and the names and ages of their employees' children? Sadly, too often, leaders struggle with this. Yet as leaders, one of our primary responsibilities is to actively build strong rapport with our employees.

Even what appears to be a little thing to us may be huge to younger team members—their first car, for example. Do you remember your first car? John admits his was a total beater that shouldn't have been allowed on the road; however, it was all his. Getting that car was more special to him than driving a fancier car off the showroom floor years later.

The Ripple Effect of Positive Work Conversations

It's not just how much we talk about work, but the content and tone of those discussions. Positive workplace conversations not only enhance the individual's outlook but also create a ripple effect that influences the wider community's perception of a company. When employees feel engaged, valued, and part of something meaningful, they become ambassadors of the brand, unconsciously marketing the organization's values and mission.

Beyond the immediate social circle, the power of digital media cannot be overstated. Today, a casual conversation about work can quickly be shared, retweeted, or reposted, amplifying its reach exponentially. Platforms such as LinkedIn, where employees often share their achievements and company updates, can spread the message even further. These shared positive sentiments build an organization's reputation and can attract not just potential customers, but also top-tier talent.

The Importance of Authenticity

While structured sound bites for new employees can help provide a clear message, fostering an environment where employees organically speak positively about their work is essential. Authentic, spontaneous conversations about job satisfaction and company culture have a genuine tone that is often more relatable and impactful. These unscripted moments, born from genuine satisfaction and pride in one's job, truly resonate with listeners.

Empowerment through Knowledge

Additionally, to empower employees both new and old, make sure they have a clear understanding of the company's goals, vision, and accomplishments. When they can see the bigger picture, they can find their place in it and take pride in being part of something larger than themselves. Regular updates about the company's achievements, innovations, and milestones can be a source of pride and a topic of positive conversation.

While the frequency with which we talk about work is notable, the quality of these conversations is paramount. Leaders have the responsibility and the privilege to shape these discussions, turning them into powerful tools for brand building and employee engagement. Investing in genuine, meaningful interactions and fostering a culture of pride and belonging will ensure that when your employees talk about work, they do so with enthusiasm and authenticity.

Leading from a Distance

In our new virtual labor force, leaders need to know how to lead from a distance, to help their employees feel emotionally and professionally connected, along with promoting a sense of collaboration and work community. This was hard enough when we had all our employees under one roof. Now the goal posts have moved. Without an emotional connection to the brand, their leaders, and the feeling that the work they do provides meaning and purpose, employees will be unengaged and a flight risk for a "better offer."

> "Leadership is not about being in charge. Leadership is about taking care of those in your charge."
> —Simon Sinek

How to Create Virtual Energy and Make an Emotional Connection with Your Team

In the new reality, most businesses realize they have to offer hybrid, flexible, work-from-home (WFH) models to their employees. There are several negative side effects of working from home, such as employees feeling emotionally neglected and professionally isolated, as well as a lack of energy, collaboration, and sense of work community.

An amazing best practice we have found that addresses these potential issues is what we like to call the "Team Rally," which can be held once a week, every other week, or monthly. This is done on a virtual platform (e.g., Zoom) and can last anywhere from 30 to 90 minutes. The more often you do them, the shorter they can be. We recommend small teams no larger than 12 employees. The following is an example of The DiJulius Group's agenda for our Team Rally.

Let us clarify a few of the not-so-obvious items on the agenda.

- Point number 6 from Image 6.1: Discuss one thing from our Credo Card. (See Image 6.2 and 6.3.) We focus on one item—it could be our Customer Service Action Statement, one of the three pillars, or a never and always. We then give examples of how we execute it in our daily interactions with our clients.

- Point number 7 from Image 6.1: Employee FORD Trivia. We share FORDs and guess which employee we are talking about.

WEEKLY TEAM RALLY AGENDA

1. One word opener	(All)	30 seconds
2. Milestones & celebrations	(Host)	3 minutes
3. Top 3 priorities	(All)	5 minutes
4. Client headlines	(All)	3 minutes
5. Credo Card	(Host)	3 minutes
6. FORD Trivia	(Host)	3 minutes
7. "Give More" shout outs	(All)	5 minutes
8. At Your Service	(All)	5 minutes
9. Parking lot	(All)	15 minutes
10. Big Talk	(All)	15 minutes

Image 6.1

KNOW MORE

Provide resources
Advise brilliantly
Anticipate needs

CARE MORE

Build meaningful relationships
Create memorable experiences
Know their FORD

GIVE MORE

Surprise and delight
Whatever/Whenever
Exceed expectation

**CUSTOMER
EXPERIENCE ACTION
STATEMENT**

Carpe Momento

Know More | Care More | Give More

Image 6.2

NEVER(S)

1. Point
2. Say "No"
3. Say "No problem"
4. Cold transfer
5. Say "I don't know"
6. Assume
7. Show frustration
8. Make excuses or overshare
9. Deliver bad news electronically
10. Leave things to chance

ALWAYS

1. Show
2. Offer what you can do
3. Say "Certainly, my pleasure, absolutely"
4. Warm transfer
5. Find out
6. Manage expectations
7. Be on stage
8. Own and take care of it
9. Have a conversation
10. Be prepared

Image 6.3

GUESS WHO

1. Who played soccer in college?

2. Whose nickname was Stinky?

3. Who has an identical twin?

4. Who was arrested for skinny dipping in high school?

5. Whose dream is it to swim with dolphins?

- Point number 8 from Image 6.1: "Give More" shout outs. Every employee in the virtual meeting must recognize one team member, who is also in the meeting, for giving more in their job, going above and beyond for a team member, a client, or the company.

- Point number 9 from Image 6.1: At Your Service. We find out who needs any help, advice, or expertise on something they are working on. We don't discuss or help during the Team Rally; we just coordinate who can help and they take it offline.

- Point number 10 from Image 6.1: Parking Lot. Things that need to be discussed, shared, or asked of the rest of the team that didn't apply to the earlier agenda.

- Point number 11 from Image 6.1: Big Talk questions. A student at Northwestern University, Kalina Silvermana, created the Big Talk game to intentionally get people to have more meaningful conversations. We ask each employee one deep question that results in a thoughtful answer, which gives insight about each team member to the rest of the team. Examples of Big Talk questions we ask are:

- If you died today, what would have been your biggest regret?

- What achievement from your childhood are you most proud of?

- What keeps you up at night?

- Who do/did you respect the most in life and why?

- If you could change one thing in your life right now, what would it be?

- What was the biggest obstacle you have had to overcome?

Many of the answers are surprising. Several people get emotional. Most of all we find out a lot more about each other, even though many of us have known each other and worked closely together for more than a decade.

Whether your team is working virtually or in person, the Team Rally is a fantastic exercise to:

- Build stronger emotional connections with coworkers and their leaders

- Help humanize each person

- Bring more energy, collaboration, and a sense of work community

- Tie employees' roles directly to the company's sense of purpose

Want Stronger Employee Engagement? Engage Their Families

The foundation of every great culture is built on strong leaders who constantly recognize their employees' contributions. However, when Dave Timmons was the SVP at Bank of America, he took employee recognition to another level. In his book, *Ways to Roll Out the Red Carpet for Your Customers*, he says, "I asked one of my team members to head a special two-month-long project. She finished the project under budget, way ahead of schedule, and exceeded my expectations. So, I wanted to do something special to thank her."

Timmons used a special form to get to know team members, asking them to share ten of their favorite things (food, restaurant, shopping center, and so on) or some of their firsts (first car, first concert, and so on). "I knew this team member had a sports team she liked and particular places she liked to shop. However, I wanted to make this recognition extra special because she really deserved it."

Timmons goes on, "About a month after she completed the project, a letter showed up in this team member's mailbox addressed to her husband, Roger, and their three children, Emily, Shaun, and Katrina. It read, 'Dear Roger, Emily, Shaun, and Katrina: I want to tell you how special your wife and mother is. She just finished a project, and she is so appreciated at our company that I wanted you to know two things: First, how proud we are of her and how appreciative I am to you for allowing her to take time away from you to work for us. On behalf of our entire team and me, please surprise her with this gift certificate from Ann Taylor Loft, because we know that's where she likes to shop. Sincerely, Dave Timmons, Senior Vice President.'"

Timmons explains, "When you engage the people employees care about, like their family, in their success, you hit a double home run. You can reward them with something—and that's good. But if you want to go for the real wow, try to include their family. It especially gives the kids something nice to remember."

At John Robert's Spa, one of John's favorite moments is seeing an employee get promoted onto the floor as a full-time hairdresser. This usually happens after about 6 to 12 months of intense training and assisting. The leaders at JR make the event special. The promotion is kept a secret to the employee getting promoted. While they are at work, out of nowhere, we may ask them to go get something out of a certain room. When they walk into that room, a crowd of people is there to surprise them. The group is made up of coworkers, parents, friends, and/or a significant other. There are always plenty of hugs, smiles, and tears.

John Ruhlin, in his book *Giftology*, underscores the importance of family by sharing something an early mentor told him: "All of my clients are married, and I find that if I take care of the family, everything else seems to take care of itself." Inspired by that idea, Ruhlin has implemented his own employee benefit: "Treating our employees well is a top priority, which is why we pay to have their houses cleaned every other week. Happy employees have happy families."[8]

Another best practice is leaders writing thank-you notes to spouses and/or parents, telling them what amazing contributions and impact their family member is making to the organization.

Chief Fun Officer

It has long been recognized that all work and no play is likely to lead to less productive, dissatisfied workers. Aspects of human nature, such as relationships, are important motivating factors in workplace culture.

"Unhappy people are in survival mode. Their brains are unable to create and innovate when they're in such states," says Rebecca Binnendyk, a coach who helps companies improve employee morale. "So, how can they even begin to be productive or increase their profits from this state of mind? If individuals are not reaching their potential the company as a whole will not reach their potential either. The truth is most employees are not functioning even close to their capacity because they're just plain unhappy."

Binnendyk continues, "People are recognizing that life is short and that much of their lives are spent at work. They are beginning to see the value in working with people they enjoy being around, and being in a space that appreciates them. Many are even willing to take lower pay in exchange for feeling valued, seen, and heard."[9]

Do you have a CFO? We don't mean chief financial officer; we mean chief fun officer. Every company needs one. It doesn't have to be a salaried position, nor does it have to be someone from management. It also can be a team of CFOs—one from each department or location. Team members love to be part of a committee that helps plan team and company events.

Most companies that are not in the Fortune 500 can't replicate office perks such as music and art studios, mini-golf courses, ping-pong tables, foosball, rock climbing walls, on-site day cares, health clinics, and even nap pods. And all of that was prior to the WFH era, so those extravagant perks are no longer seen as benefits.

Fun in the workplace (virtually or in person) can also foster more positive attitudes, help teams become more cohesive, and assist people in dealing with or recovering from stressful work experiences, while also developing stronger relationships.

Fun Isn't Just for Employees

Employees are also likely to partake in festivities if they see their leaders are involved. This helps humanize the leader and allows for a connection away from the boss/employee scenario.

Now more than ever, we need to find reasons to get together— little outings, celebrations, potluck lunches, holiday parties, happy hour get-togethers, a night at the ball game, or a community fundraiser.

Ask who on your team would love to be a CFO and bring more fun to your organization on a regular basis.

Care for Your Employees and Their Personal Development

For your team members to be at their best, it goes without saying that you, as a leader, need to be at your best. In addition to building strong businesses, the best leaders help employees reach their full potential. This is the game changer. Much of what we have already discussed in this chapter, good companies do to create stronger workplace culture. Demonstrating that as a leader you care about your team members as human beings who have lives outside their careers versus only the value they can bring to the bottom line of your organization is what will separate you and make your company legendary in their minds. It is what will make them become brand evangelists of your company to everyone they interact with: customers, team members, potential team members, family, and friends.

Train the Whole Person

We need to be the type of company that helps employees live extraordinary lives. How? We must start with investing in and training the whole person, not just providing the professional development that makes them more productive and profitable for our business.

Surprisingly, you can train the whole person extremely inexpensively simply by providing resources for your employees to take advantage of. Sometimes one of our leaders or team members might be the in-house expert on a topic and can provide a one-hour class to other employees. Other times we bring in an outside local expert, for instance a mortgage lender, money manager, or health and fitness trainer, whom we don't have to pay because they have an opportunity to pick up potential new clients. These classes are optional for whoever feels they can benefit from them.

> **"Work can provide the opportunity for spiritual, personal, and financial growth. If it doesn't, we are wasting far too much of our lives on it."**
> **—James Autry, author**

Focusing on the Five Fs

The best place to start in providing resources for the whole person is with the Five Fs. The Five Fs are commonly the top New Year's resolutions that people are trying to improve:

1. Finances

2. Fitness

3. Family

4. Faith

5. Fun

FINANCES

- A class on how to purchase their first or next home
- Financial planning (investing, saving for college, retirement)
- Money management and budgeting

FITNESS

- Living a healthier lifestyle
- Weight loss
- Getting in better shape
- Yoga
- Meditation
- Avoiding burnout and stress
- Recommended apps for sleep and stress reduction

FAMILY

- Parenting
- Stronger relationships
- Recognizing and helping family members with stress and burnout

FAITH

- This is not about religion but about helping your employees (and ourselves) maintain a positive state of mind about the world today and in their life

- Best practices to proactively stay in a positive mindset
- Avoiding doomscrolling
- Avoiding black hole conversations
- Navigating divisive topics

FUN

- Team socials
- Themed workdays
- Organized lunches
- Suggestions for seasonal events (concerts, theater, sports, etc.)
- Family activities

ADDITIONAL RESOURCES

- Goal setting
- Personal time management
- Curing procrastination
- Managing your to-do lists
- Offering and organizing book clubs on many of these topics

Prioritizing Employee Mental Well-Being

Another silver lining that came out of the pandemic is that it is now more acceptable to admit you may struggle with your mental well-being. Building a world-class employee experience culture means you make sure you don't leave out the critical component of employee mental wellness.

Today's leaders need to know how to recognize and support their employees' mental well-being. They need to be aware of the direct and indirect dangers to your team members when they don't have the support they need. This doesn't mean leaders need to turn into therapists. But organizations and their leaders better be more than just empathetic; they must build cultures that support and provide resources, both preventive and reactive, for employees struggling with their mental wellness.

Organizations provide their employees with medical, vision, and dental insurance. But what about mental health benefits? Many companies leave this out of the package. Meaning the wealthy, who can afford to pay out of pocket for mental health care, are typically the only ones who get access. Mental wellness cannot be a privilege for a small percentage of our population; it must be accessible for everyone.

A New Leadership Approach to Modern Health in the Workplace

We have seen an increasing number of high-profile athletes and entertainers speak out about their struggles with mental well-being. These awareness campaigns are a great start. However, few business leaders have done the same. Why? There's a lingering stigma associated with revealing such seeming vulnerability at work. But burnout, anxiety, and depression among workers is hitting record levels. According to a report from mental health consultancy Mind Share Partners, three-quarters of full-time US workers reported experiencing at least one symptom of a mental health condition.[10]

The mental health of America's younger population was a major national concern before the pandemic. Now it has reached crisis stage. In a 2022 survey by the American Psychological Association, 67 percent of people reported feeling anxious or depressed in the prior month.[11] What's more, by some estimates, half of Americans will experience an issue with significant symptoms and the negative impact of mental illness over their lifetime. The need for employee assistance programs and mental health initiatives has never been greater.

Progress toward Mental Health Legislation for Employees and Their Families

Lawmakers are wrestling with how to ensure that mental health and physical health are treated equally by employers and insurers. Up until recently, mental health has long been considered a taboo topic in many workplaces. However, the Great Resignation era taught us that now, more than ever, addressing mental health in the workplace has become a business imperative. "As a nation, it's past time to provide people with the support they need. And employers have a significant role to play," wrote Garen Staglin in a *Forbes* article titled "It's Time for Employers to Support Youth Mental Health." "For starters," Staglin points out, "young people are the sons and daughters of current employees."[12]

The mental health of our employees' children can have a direct, sometimes negative impact on our workplace environments. The answer lies in providing appropriate mental health resources. We must make employee health, on all levels, a high priority and show it by offering well-being benefits in addition to traditional health insurance.

Fast Company brought together a group of successful CEOs, entertainers, and subject matter experts to discuss what needs to be done around employee mental wellness awareness. In the magazine's "Mental Health at Work: It's (Finally) Time to Talk about It," Amit Paley, CEO of the Trevor Project, the world's largest suicide prevention and crisis intervention organization for LGBTQ young people, says, "It is so important that people know that it is okay not to be okay. When we're not feeling that way, it's important to talk about it and share that with other people." Paley points out that the workplace used to be where an employee would set their personal life aside during work hours, in a sense, temporarily shutting down part of their humanity. This rarely leads to healthy work environments. Currently there is an evolution toward a new model where people can more fully brings themselves to work. Being human is good business.

To Paley's insights, serial entrepreneur Paul English adds, "Secrecy and shame are the enemies of healing. I think the main responsibility we have as business leaders, when it comes to mental health—and really all health issues—is to let your team know . . . that you'll be there for them when they're struggling."[13]

English shares that when his team sees his own vulnerability, they can feel more comfortable sharing their issues without the worry of mental health stigma. Confidence may get people to follow, but vulnerability engenders loyalty. Employees helping employees in the workplace needs to start with the leaders. When issues come up outside the workplace and employees feel that management cares about them and their families, they can function better in all areas of life.

Invest In Employee Well-Being

We believe you will see larger organizations such as Fortune 500 companies start providing comprehensive, affordable, and age-appropriate mental health care for all employees and their families. This will include no- or low-cost access to mental health services, as well as implementing policies that help employees address mental health challenges, both at home and in the workplace, such as more paid family and sick leave.

Happier, Healthier Employees Stick Around

Supporting employee mental well-being is not only about being altruistic. Mental health investments are good for company culture and for productivity; by some estimates, for every one dollar invested in supporting mental health in the workplace, there is a four dollar payback.[14] That is a powerfully positive ROI! With improvements over time as we all fight to lead in the great employee retention of talented workforce, mental well-being will be a leading tool for attracting and keeping employees—especially younger employees. It is no longer a perk, but rather a must-have and will be reflected in your company's retention rates and employee morale.

Whether you recognize it or not, every company in America is impacted by the mental health crisis. By taking targeted action to support mental health challenges, organizations will reap the benefits now and for decades to come. Not only will it be a relationship builder, greatly increasing employee satisfaction and employee well-being, it will help create a stronger, healthier, more compassionate society.

The US Surgeon General Declares Loneliness an Epidemic

US Surgeon General Dr. Vivek H. Murthy released an advisory on how the "epidemic of loneliness and isolation" is negatively impacting millions of people across the country. "In recent years, about one in two adults in America reported experiencing loneliness," White House press secretary Karine Jean-Pierre said when the advisory was released. "And that was before the COVID-19 pandemic cut off so many of us from friends, loved ones, and support systems."[15] It's not surprising the surgeon general has declared loneliness an epidemic.

The research on this public health crisis is sobering. Studies have demonstrated that loneliness and isolation are linked to major health conditions: inflammation; immune changes; pain; insomnia; mental health issues such as depression, anxiety, self-harm, and suicidality; and higher risks of heart disease, stroke, diabetes, addiction, dementia, and premature death.[16]

The surgeon general's advisory shares that social connection is as essential to humanity as food, water, or shelter. All people are wired for human connection. "Given the profound consequences of loneliness and isolation, we have an opportunity, and an obligation, to make the same investments in addressing social connection that we have made in addressing tobacco use, obesity, and the addiction crisis," Murthy says in his advisory. He believes "the social fabric of our nation" can be repaired if all members and segments of society band together. This includes people and their families, the communities in which they live and the places in which they work and worship, educational institutions, healthcare systems, tech companies, and public health organizations removing the stigma around loneliness and improving how our policies and culture act in response to it. We need to make broader efforts to rebuild a culture of connection, healthy relationships, and collective well-being.[17]

The epidemic of loneliness is only getting worse. Help team members find their tribe. Connect deeply. Seek out those who are on the fringes and show them love. How leaders treat their team members when they are going through difficult situations in their lives is what they remember forever. Employees want something to brag about. Let them brag about how amazing their boss and company was during their difficult times.

Helping Your Employees Find Their Ikigai

On Japan's Okinawa Island, nicknamed the "island of longevity," locals refuse to die. A highly unusual percentage of seniors on Okinawa Island live a healthy life past the age of 100. Locals enjoy low levels of heart disease, cancer, and dementia, and a robust social life. Their secret is *ikigai*.

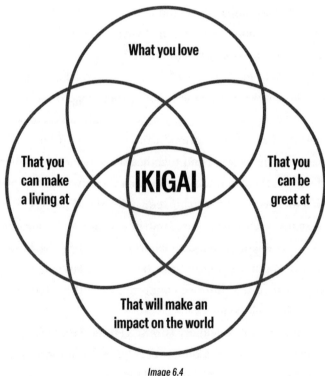

Image 6.4

In Japanese culture, it is believed that when you have discovered your calling, that thing that makes you happy to get out of bed every day and get busy, you have found your ikigai. One's ikigai is found at the intersection of four areas:

1. Find something you love to do

2. That you can excel at

3. That you can make a great living at

4. That makes a positive impact on the world

Finding something you enjoy doing but you can't be a master at is a hobby. Finding something you are excellent at that you do not love doing is known as a job.

The first place to start with the ikigai exercise is using it as a compass for finding your company's purpose. But it shouldn't stop there. If you want long-term successful leaders committed to your brand, you must help your leaders find their ikigai within your organization. Otherwise, all your company will be is a resume builder.

Now, as leaders, it is important that we get to know our employees as individuals. Only then can we most effectively guide them to positions in our companies that will best suit them and allow for their greatest growth. This guidance not only can help employees start out on the ideal career path, but it can also aid established team members in transitioning to roles for which they are better suited and in which they will find fresh inspiration. Equally importantly, it can phase out workers who may need to leave your organization and possibly even your industry. The healthiest company cultures have employees who find joy and purpose in their work, knowing their leaders have their personal, not just professional, interests at heart.

Share the Stories of Team Members
You Helped Successfully Move On

In earlier chapters, we discussed how important it is to constantly be sharing your organization's "rags to riches" stories, such as how a team member who started out in an entry-level position, at the time thinking it was going to be a temporary transitional job, rose through the ranks, and their efforts and loyalty were rewarded; today, they are one of your success stories. While that is important, maybe just as important are the stories of the team members you helped successfully move on from your organization.

Do your leaders know what your employees' five-year goals are? Especially the ones who don't see themselves working in your company five years from now? Help them obtain their goals; let that story go viral. For one, they will be much better team members while they work at your company. Second, they will be brand evangelists for potential employees and customers. And third, it will demonstrate that your leaders truly care about the human being versus how much productivity can they squeeze out of each employee.

Leaders who care about their employees and work for their employees rather than thinking that their employees work for them will disproportionately attract and retain top talent.

> "What a great honor and responsibility, to be a fundamental reason why people accomplish more, enjoy more, and are more fulfilled in the one life they have to live."

Imagine having a culture of team members similar to the people of Okinawa—team members who are often so inspired and energized that they'll put off retirement so they can keep enjoying their calling in life.

A Company That Offers Lifetime Employment

Next Jump is renowned for its employee discount platform, extensively utilized by over 70 percent of Fortune 1000 companies to aid their employees in saving money. The company goes beyond offering discounts; it provides a suite of applications and tools designed to assess and enhance employee performance and the overall culture within an organization. A standout feature of Next Jump is its commitment to providing lifetime employment to its workforce.

At its core, Next Jump prioritizes company culture and personal growth above all else, famously adopting a policy of lifelong employment where employees are not terminated due to performance issues. Founded in 1994 by Charlie Kim, the company is based in New York and has grown to employ over 200 people, extending its presence with offices in Boston, San Francisco, and London.

In recognition of its unique approach to employee development, Next Jump was identified as one of three Deliberately Developmental Organizations (DDOs) in the book *An Everyone Culture* by Robert Kegan and Lisa Lahey. DDOs are a rare breed of companies. They focus heavily on nurturing company culture, personal and professional development, self-organization, lifelong learning, and transparency. For firms like Next Jump, the connection between profits and employee development is clear and pivotal; the higher the skill and engagement level of the employees, the greater the reliability and size of profits.

> **"If you had hard times in your family, would you ever consider laying off one of your children?"**
> **—Charlie Kim, CEO of Next Jump**

Next Jump's Culture Formula

Next Jump believes the way to become a better company is by employees working on themselves and, in turn, helping others grow. At the heart of Next Jump's culture and management philosophy is the following formula:

BETTER ME + BETTER YOU = BETTER US

IMPROVE YOURSELF → HELP OTHERS

At Next Jump, those employees who improve the culture the most reap the highest financial rewards. As the authors Kegan and Lahey share in their book, "At Next Jump, you could be a revenue-generating god and still be penalized in compensation if you're not working on personal growth. The biggest bonus and salary increases go to those who improve the culture."[18]

A Business with No Brilliant Jerks Allowed

Next Jump doesn't want to be a company of "brilliant jerks." Their number one hiring criterion is humility, as they believe this is the most important predictor of personal growth. Coachability, responsibility, and absence of victim mentality are other key characteristics.

Next Jump has developed the Feedback Lab app, which allows every employee to give anonymous, public feedback to everyone else. "Just imagine what that does to transparency and open debate. True, in [the corporate culture of] most traditional organizations, it could be humiliating to be criticized publicly by your colleagues," Charlie Kim shares in a blog. "And yes, you may have a troll who will badmouth everything you do. But the idea itself is fascinating because it puts the money where many companies' mouth is."[19]

At Next Jump, accountability is forced to unprecedented levels for all employees. In such an environment, criticizing someone higher on the ladder is now all but risk-free. Old-school pep talks and cryptic instructions no longer fly when everyone across an entire organization—including senior-level employees—is open to public assessment.

A Zero-Risk Employer

Next Jump introduced its No Firing Policy in 2012—offering a commitment of lifetime employment for its employees—"The ultimate safety at work," says Tarun Gidoomal, former managing director at Next Jump. "Aside from increasing our hiring standards, this was a signal of intent for employees to show that you can expose vulnerabilities, weaknesses, and faults without the fear of losing your job."[20] Such powerful words. This employment-for-life policy forces Next Jump to put even more effort into finding the right talent and to go to great lengths to support employees when they struggle. When employees feel their employer has their back, any woe-is-me attitude tends to go out the window. And if that isn't enough, when employees are treated with such empathy in their workplace, it naturally translates to the empathy they extend to customers, which tends to result in best-in-class customer service. Everyone wins.

Turnover Down, Revenue and Profitability Up

Gidoomal says the company's sales have increased by five times, over $2.5 billion annually, since launching the lifetime employment policy. They have also seen an impact of this business strategy on other metrics such as profitability and retention of leadership. The company's example of direct correlation between the achievement of personal goals and long-term professional success has the US Air Force, the CIA, and many corporate companies studying Next Jump culture strategies.

A Leader in the Employee Experience Revolution

Chick-fil-A says its service is so consistent because it invests more than other companies in training its employees and helping them advance their careers—regardless of whether those careers are in fast food. The company genuinely cares about creating emotional bonds with its employees.

Leaders are encouraged to ask their new hires what their career goals are and then to try to help them achieve those goals. "Do you know the dreams of your team?" leaders are constantly asked. For Kevin Moss, a Chick-fil-A manager of over 20 years, supporting his team has meant funding an employee's marketing degree and paying for another worker to take photography classes. Moss says he also tries to support his employees in times of need. For example, if an employee's family member is in the hospital, he will send food to the family and hospital staff. "I've found people are more motivated and respond better when you care about them," Moss told *Business Insider* in 2016.[21] Another strong example of the phrase "being human is good business."

This best-in-class customer experience–leading company also offers, in all its restaurants, leadership positions that come with higher pay as well as greater responsibilities. Crew members can work their way toward "director" positions in marketing, cleanliness, kitchen operations, and drive-thru operations. "The better we train, the longer people stay with us," Moss says.[22] It is a smart strategy focused on bringing out the best in people, so that the best can then be offered.

How Chick-fil-A Gets Their Young Workforce to Deliver a World-Class Experience

How are certain businesses able to scale and still maintain business excellence to their customers and their employees? One of our favorite leaders we have worked with is Ryan Magnon, senior principal operations lead at Chick-fil-A corporate. Ryan has an amazing hospitality pedigree, having worked with two of the biggest hospitality legends: Horst Schulze, cofounder of The Ritz-Carlton, and Truett Cathy, founder of Chick-fil-A. Ryan shares some valuable insights into the amazing cultures he has worked in.

Quality Attracts Quality

"It's not just about going out and finding great team members. It's starting with a nucleus of quality leaders. When leaders identify with the company values, they are more likely to create an environment for their team members and attract team members that also value that," says Magnon.[23]

Once You Become a Leader, You Lose the Right to Make Excuses

This is one of our favorites quotes we learned from Ryan: "Horst Schulze told me, 'Once you become a leader, all responsibility for results is yours, regardless of the reason for those results.'" Magnon's spin on that is "When you transition from being a team member to being a leader, you go from being cared for to being the one who cares for within an organization. You are now responsible for other people and for making sure things are done the right way. Responsibility doesn't fall to the team member— it rises to the leader. Who selected them, oriented them, trained them, or determines the best role they should be in? The leader."[24]

The Three Questions You Need to Ask Employees About Their Leaders

Want to know how well a leader is doing at creating high employee morale? Ask employees to rank their direct leader on the following three questions using a scale of 1 to 5 (5 being the highest):

1. Does this leader care about the company?

2. Does this leader care about my success?

3. Does this leader care about me as a person?

Perception is reality. If the average score from your employees is less than a 4.5 for any of these three questions, you have work to do—and it will be clear in which area.

Conduct Stay Interviews

Stay interviews can be a valuable tool for improving employee retention and engagement. Unlike exit interviews, which are conducted after an employee has decided to leave an organization, stay interviews are conducted with current employees, typically those considered to be high performing or high potential.

The purpose of stay interviews is to understand what motivates and engages employees and what might cause them to leave. This information can then be used to create strategies to increase employee satisfaction and retention. By addressing concerns and understanding employee needs while they are still with the company, organizations can make timely changes to help retain key talent. It also sends a message to employees that their opinions and satisfaction matter to the company, potentially fostering greater loyalty and engagement.

Why One-On-One Meetings Can't Be Optional

Typically, when we are consulting with an organization, two things are happening when it comes to one-on-one meetings.

1. They are not happening at all.
2. They are not happening well.

Meetings Not Happening at All

One-on-one meetings are one of those things that organizations need their leaders to understand are a priority and a necessity. If not, these meetings on the calendar easily get bumped as "more important" items pop up. Since one-on-one meetings are not "revenue generating" or "client facing," they are often seen as a less important use of time, or worse, even optional. Nothing could be further from the truth.

Here is some data to back up the point that managers do not make one-on-one meetings a priority: A study conducted by the organization Hypercontext states that while 94 percent of managers claim to schedule one-on-one meetings with their teams, employees report less than half of those meetings actually take place—or roughly 45 to 50 percent get canceled.[25]

Many leaders in the call center industry have learned the importance of effective one-on-one meetings for employee engagement and tenure. Length of tenure can be particularly important in a call center environment. To make sure that one-on-ones do not fall by the wayside, many organizations have made holding these meetings mandatory and go the extra step by making sure each manager has enough time in their day to conduct them—often reassigning other tasks that might get in the way.[26]

Meetings Not Happening Well

A good one-on-one meeting can boost employee engagement, morale, and productivity. A poorly done one-on-one can do just the opposite. Because of this, we need to ensure that our leaders understand the importance of this meeting and have the training to conduct an effective one-on-one meeting. A mistake so many organizations make is that they want to begin this initiative and ask their leaders to conduct these meetings, but they never provide training on how to conduct an effective one-on-one. And that is how so many organizations have unproductive and even harmful one-on-one meetings taking place.

90 Percent Listening, 10 Percent Talking

So, let's start by defining some important elements of an effective one-on-one meeting. According to Qualtrics, the two most important actions in one-on-one meetings are listening and clarification. Qualtrics states that the manager should be doing 90 percent of the listening and only 10 percent of the talking, making sure that all aspects of the job are clear.[27] Think of the one-on-one meetings taking place in your organization right now. Are the managers following the 90 percent listening/10 percent talking rule? One thing needs to be clear on holding one-on-ones—it is the employee's meeting. It is not the time for the manager to share all their issues and frustrations. Managers must remember that the primary goal and benefit of effective one-on-one meetings is to build trust with employees while improving engagement, productivity, and performance. A *Harvard Business Review* study showed that employees who receive little to no one-on-one time with their managers are less engaged with their work and the organization.[28]

Tips and Tricks to Deliver Effective One-on-Ones in Your Organization

1. Let the team member set the agenda—and make it collaborative. Topics typically include current goals, career aspirations, and positive recognition, all of which can be ongoing topics.

2. Keep it informal—one-on-ones do not always have to take place across a desk. Go for a walk or head to the coffee shop.

3. Think of it less as a meeting and more as an ongoing discussion. Track items discussed for progress and resolution.

4. Make it a regular occurrence. Schedule one-on-one meetings in advance and stick to the schedule. Do not cancel this meeting unless there are no other alternatives. Canceling sends a message that this meeting is not important.

5. Create a template for consistency and train managers to use it. It is very important to make sure that one-on-ones are not only happening consistently, but are also consistently conducted well. A simple template can ensure your managers are following a path to success.

The following images (6.5, 6.6, and 6.7) are some examples of one-on-one templates our clients use:

IMAGE 6.5: ONE-ON-ONE MEETING AGENDA

Employee:

Date:

Topic	Time	Notes
Informal catch-up	5 minutes	
Employee's concerns	10 minutes	
Your notes/comments	10 minutes	
Action planning	5 minutes	

IMAGE 6.6: ONE-ON-ONE MEETING

Alpin Haus

Name:	Date:

PERSONAL	ACTION ITEMS
Things going well:	
Goals & progress:	

PROFESSIONAL	ACTION ITEMS
Things going well:	
Goals & progress:	

IMAGE 6.7: ONE-ON-ONE MEETING DOCUMENT

Team Member:		Team/Position:	
Date Updated:		Team Leader:	
Meeting Date:		Last Meeting Date:	

Team Member to complete worksheet and provide to Team Leader for Individual Touchbase discussion.

ACTIVITIES AND UPDATES

Successes Since Last Meeting	Focus for Next Week/Month/Quarter
Current Challenges/Area for Improvement	Solutions

PERSONAL GROWTH/ DEVELOPMENT GOAL(S) & PROGRESS UPDATE	MEASUREMENT OF SUCCESS	COMPLETION DATE

GOALS (NEW/UPDATE)	MEASUREMENT OF SUCCESS	COMPLETION DATE

Praise Publicly, Reprimand Privately in the Digital World

Chances are good you have heard "praise publicly, reprimand privately." As a matter of fact, its origins date back to 35 BC and writer Publilius Syrus. But have you even thought about why you should not reprimand in public? It is not just because it can embarrass a team member and start to erode trust.

Kim Scott, author of *Radical Candor*, points out that public criticism naturally causes a defensive reaction. Once in the defensive mode, it is much harder for the person to accept they have made a mistake and much harder for them to learn from the mistake.[29] Criticizing publicly is not only bad form, but it is also counterproductive. After all, mistakes are our best learning opportunity. Why would we want to stifle the learning process?

This is an area that managers and all leaders need to keep in mind as technology continues to change the landscape of our office environments and how we conduct business. Platforms like Microsoft Teams and Slack are great for maintaining communication within an organization and can allow us to quickly give a positive shout-out to a team member in front of the entire organization in a matter of seconds. The flipside is that we can just as quickly "call out" or admonish a team member in front of the entire organization.

This important leadership principle that has been around for over 2,050 years needs to be adapted to our new digital age and remain top of mind for all leaders.

7

TEARING DOWN SILOS BY BUILDING COLLABORATION ACROSS DEPARTMENTS

Creating World-Class Teamwork

Picture yourself in this situation: You are not feeling well, your chest is feeling tight and knotted, and your breathing feels off. You have a busy day and places to be, but you know something is not right. You head to the ER. At the emergency room, you have a long wait to be seen, but once you are in a room, medical personnel take great care of you. They get you into a bed and begin observations. They deem your issues to be minor and caught in time but want to keep you for observation. They let you know you will probably be in the hospital for two to three days for tests and to make sure everything is okay. Once you get to your room, the nursing team is amazing, and the doctors check on you often. You feel better and you feel well cared for. Other than the inconvenience of having to miss some things that were on your calendar and the long ER wait, you are feeling good and relieved.

Then comes your last morning. You are up early, as the overnight nurse comes in to check on you before her shift ends. She wishes you well as she lets you know that you will most likely be discharged today. In your mind you feel a sudden sense of relief. It is currently 6:00 a.m., and you envision yourself out of there by 10:00 a.m. and home for lunch. You call your spouse and ask them to take the morning off from work to come pick you up and get you home.

Then, you wait, and wait, and wait. Hospital staff comes and goes throughout the morning. No one has any information to share. The next thing you know it is 11:30 a.m. and lunch is brought in. You pass because you are still certain you will be having lunch at home. You continue to wait. Your spouse becomes antsy because they only took half a day off and need to head in soon. You ring your call button and wait some more. Finally, someone enters your room and explains that being discharged can take a long time, and that typically 4:00 or 5:00 p.m. is standard for a patient release. At this point, you are tired, hungry, and upset. You thought you were going to be home for a good chunk of the day, and now you will be lucky to make it home for dinner.

Then you start to wonder—why didn't anyone tell you? Why didn't someone take the time to set your expectations of the process and the day? The scenario described above takes place in hospitals every day—and was happening at Flagler Hospital numerous times a day. Flagler Hospital is a leading health-care provider located in historic St. Augustine, Florida. Flagler Hospital has been taking care of the community since 1889. When this scenario did occur, an otherwise wonderful experience of care would be lost, and the patient and family could only focus on this subpar last impression.

This unorganized and undercommunicated interaction was easily taking the patient, who would have been a promoter, and making them a detractor. Such scenarios obviously had negative effects on hospital satisfaction scores and social media reviews, and even resulted in an official grievance being filed from time to time. Keep in mind, this is also the last impression—which often is as important if not more important than the ever so popular first impression. In this example from Flagler Hospital, assumptions were being made by team members that someone else was sharing the important information. Or, in some cases, medical staff might have been avoiding an unpleasant conversation. Either way, the patient was left in the dark and frustrated. We will discuss what Flagler did to alleviate this major pain point, but first let's discuss what creating a world-class internal culture looks like.

The Customer Experience Is Won and Lost in the Transitions

Anytime a client goes from dealing with one team member/department to another is when things can go wrong. Take, for example, when a prospective client is dealing with the salesperson during the sales process. The prospect and the salesperson bond; the prospect loves what the salesperson tells them. Now the prospect becomes a client. The salesperson goes away, and now the client is dealing with someone in operations. The client doesn't have a bond yet with this person. When the client says, "Joe [the salesperson] told me this is what I can expect," the operations person may say, "No, that isn't correct; there must have been a miscommunication. The way it will go is like this . . ." Now the client may feel like they were misled during the sales process.

When focusing on creating an internal experience between team members across departments within an organization, our six goals are to

1. Remove silos, and train compassion and empathy

2. Clarify handoffs between departments

3. Identify customer segments, and define how your work impacts others

4. Understand *all* your internal customers

5. Improve communication within departments, locations, and other teams

6. Create and improve training

We will go deeper into each one of the objectives above, but first here is a look at how this focus has evolved over the years.

ImageFIRST Transformation

In early 2016, The DiJulius Group started consulting with Image-FIRST. ImageFIRST is a privately owned health-care linen and laundry services company headquartered in King of Prussia, Pennsylvania. The company was founded in 1967 and has since grown to become a leading provider of health-care laundry and linen services in the United States.

ImageFirst's senior leadership decided to focus on the client experience as part of their overall strategy. They started with one simple change—the job title of one position. For years within their industry, an integral part of the operation was the delivery driver—and that was a position that was interchangeable between competitors; if you drove for one, you had the knowledge and experience to drive for any. Not any longer—ImageFIRST was committed to building relationships and customer advocates. Delivery drivers don't do that, but "client advocates" do. The organization committed to hiring an employee who had that ability, and then gave them the service aptitude to do precisely that. That is where The DiJulius Group came in—to help create and deliver the service aptitude.

At that time, ImageFIRST brought in roughly $32 million in annual revenue. Today, they are at $500 million and still growing. The project was overseen by industry veteran Jay Juffre, at the time ImageFIRST's chief experience officer (CXO), who is now executive vice president and chief of staff. As we were preparing to get a team together for a deep dive into the customer experience, Jay brought up the fact that many of the issues that existed within their clients' experience were things that happened behind the scenes—specifically with the sales-to-service handoff of a client. Poor communication and handoffs between these departments was common. Messages went unanswered, assumptions were made on who handled what—often leaving the client frustrated. So, during the session that was intended to be a deep dive into the client experience, we paid particular attention to a key internal process—the client handoff from sales team to service team.

The ImageFIRST Team found that several issues and missed opportunities existed. These can exist in any organization. For example, it was not unusual for there to be a cold handoff from the salesperson to the service representative. The service rep would have to start from scratch learning the customer, their preferences, their challenges, as opposed to a formal introduction from one team member to another along with vital behind-the-scenes information to help set up the service rep for success (i.e., their FORD).

It was such an aha moment in our workshop that this internal interaction between departments was so vital to the overall new client experience that it became the focus during the workshop. As a matter of fact, when we rolled out new findings to the rest of the organization, this was the area that they trained on first, despite it not being the first interaction. While it was not number one in numerical order, it was deemed number one in importance.

"At ImageFIRST, we realized the biggest opportunity to drop the ball was the handoff from sales to service when we set up a new customer," Jay shared. "Our solution was to bring in our sales and service folks at all levels and map out what the non-negotiable standards should be for every new client (and the things to avoid). Once we baked out the idea as a team, we trained every sales and service person in the country on it. The result was not only a much better working relationship between departments (no more finger pointing), but more importantly a seamless transition and much improved overall customer experience. A total win-win!"[1]

Mid-States Concrete

About a year later, when Mid-States Concrete Industries was focusing on their external customer experience, they went a step further and also examined their internal customer processes. Based in South Beloit, Illinois, Mid-States Concrete Industries was founded in 1946 and has grown to become one of the largest precast concrete manufacturers in the Midwest. Mid-States was creating standards around their complex business model that included sales, design, and production; it involved several internal handoffs along the way.

The project was overseen by the company CEO, Hagen Harker, Vice President of Sales Jeremy Olivetti, and company marketing guru Stephanie Kohl.

When they rolled out their new non-negotiable standards to the teams involved, they created a printed version that traveled from team member to team member, department to department as the customer's job followed this path. So, as a job bid went from sales to the design team for initial pricing, the printed copy of the detailed standards also went along, serving as a checklist. After the customer's project had gone through the entire process (sales, design, production, and delivery), all team members who interacted with the customer would meet for a debrief. They would discuss what service defects they had encountered and how they were able to avoid and/or address them. They confirmed that they had delivered all the non-negotiable standards for that interaction stage. If they had not, they would discuss why, and how to make sure whatever barrier existed would not get in the way again. Finally, they would review any above-and-beyond opportunities, chatting about what they were able to accomplish from the list, as well as missed opportunities. This debrief afforded them the opportunity to see firsthand how all the internal departmental interactions that were part of the process had a direct effect on the external interactions and overall customer satisfaction.[2]

Other Internal Experience Applications

Around this same time, we started to learn about some pain points that a few of our franchisee clients were experiencing. One was The Maids International (TMI). The Maids International is a franchised residential cleaning service company with headquarters located in Omaha, Nebraska. The company was founded in 1979 and has since expanded to over 190 franchise locations across the United States and Canada.

The Maids International offers a 100 percent satisfaction guarantee to its customers, ensuring that they are completely satisfied with the cleaning service they receive.

While The DiJulius Group worked with TMI, company CEO Dan Kirwan noted they had never intentionally focused on the home office experience they were delivering to their franchisees. In their model, the franchisee was an internal customer, and arguably the organization's most important customer.

A World-Class Experience Starts at the Home Office

Most leaders don't do enough to educate their home office team on how they, too, have customers—in operations, in the field, and wherever there are employees who count on them every day to deliver what they need to service their customers. Every employee and department must understand the critical part they play in creating a world-class customer experience. I am not talking about employee engagement or how likely employees are to refer a family or friend. Those are important but have more to do with how good the organization is to work for. I am talking about the experience the home office team delivers to support employees who deal with the invisible service providers in IT, marketing, human resources, accounting, maintenance, and so on.

"Improving the self-esteem of the world" is the purpose statement of Self Esteem Brands (SEB), the parent company of Anytime Fitness (the world's number one "Top Global" franchise), Waxing the City, Basecamp Fitness, and The Bar Method. Anytime Fitness operates in nearly 40 countries on seven continents and has more than three million members worldwide. Anytime Fitness has been repeatedly named "Best Place to Work," and, indeed, we haven't worked with many companies that can rival the culture created by cofounders Chuck Runyon and Dave Mortensen.

Why? One key reason is they are not solely focused on the member (customer) experience. They are equally obsessed with how their headquarters delivers a similar experience to their franchisees and team members in their 5,000-plus locations. Among other things, Anytime Fitness measures how satisfied their franchisees are with headquarters, just as they do when a member visits one of their clubs. After a franchisee has an interaction with someone at the home office, they may get an email asking them to rate the experience.

This type of accountability is crucial in changing a company's culture and revolutionizing the mindset of traditional home offices, which too often act like the people from the field or operations are an interruption. "Ongoing stakeholder feedback, consumers, franchisees, and employees, is critical for growth and turns shareholders into 'careholders,'" says Runyon.[3]

World Class Internal Culture Today

The DiJulius Group realized an opportunity existed from what these organizations needed. What we learned from working with companies like ImageFIRST, Mid-States Concrete, and The Maids International is that the same tool we used to help organizations create a consistently great customer experience could be tweaked to create a great employee experience. It did not matter if we were focusing on team members delivering service to an external customer, or a department working with another department, or a home office to a multiunit location—organizations need to create standards in order to deliver a consistent experience.

Nothing will ruin your experience faster than rapid growth!

Intermountain Health is a nonprofit health-care system based in Salt Lake City, Utah. Founded in 1975, Intermountain Health operates 24 hospitals, over 200 clinics, and has more than 40,000 employees serving communities across Utah, Idaho, and Nevada.

While working with Intermountain, we were able to assemble 45 team members representing multiple departments and locations for an internal culture exploration.

During the internal departmental workshop, one team member noted that they were in a room working with departments and team members they had never met personally (outside of some emails) yet relied on every day. Many of these team members were working in multiple locations across the region, and rarely had an opportunity to interact or meet. While Intermountain Health expanded and added locations, it did not focus on the internal culture (most organizations do not), which led to internal breakdowns like silos and employee miscommunication, with a profound negative effect on the external customer. It happens all the time. As a matter of fact, it is a quite natural part of organizational growth—but it can be prevented with some focus. The project oversight team of Vice President Nadia Khan and Vice President Jeremy Cox realized the importance of having this focus to sustain and fuel future growth.

The Intermountain Health example leads us right back to our six objectives of focus to create an internal experience between team members across departments within an organization—stated earlier in this chapter. Let's take a deeper look into all six.

1. Remove silos, and train compassion and empathy.

As that member of the Intermountain Health team so astutely noted, many seasoned team members in the room that day had never met one another. This often happens in larger organizations. And when team members do not know one another and do not understand job responsibilities, pressures, and demands of one another, silos go up. The blame game (passing the buck between departments) is much easier to play when your fellow team member is merely an email address—versus a coworker you have met.

If you are part of a smaller organization, take advantage of your size and make sure your teams that support one another know one another. You can achieve this goal through team meetings, team-building events, or virtual huddles (shared in chapter 6) for remote workers. Taking advantage of a smaller organizational size can really work to your advantage.

Larger organizations do not have that luxury. When organizations have large teams supporting large teams, more must be done to make this connection.

What can a larger organization do to help create that internal compassion and empathy? One answer is to create a day in the life of a team member. Early in the teamwork workshop process of creating a world-class internal departmental experience, we take some time to focus on what our fellow team members are dealing with on a regular basis. When we focus on the day in the life, our first goal is to educate team members about the responsibilities and challenges their coworkers and colleagues have that they may not be aware of. In addition, we also look at stressors outside of the job. That could include their coworkers' family issues, car trouble, kids' needs, and so many other things that have an outside influence on our job performance.

When we know and understand what our team members are going through, we become more patient because we realize what they have on their plate and we are willing to advocate for them. We're willing to go above and beyond. We become more appreciative of all roles and departments. We're also more willing to lend a hand to support each other.

Most DiJulius Group clients create videos of both a day in the life of their customers and a day in the life of their employees. Anytime a business creates one of these videos, they see a significant increase in employee service aptitude and empathy for their clients and coworkers. It's a great tool companies can use and share with their team on an ongoing basis.

One great example of a day in the life of a team member comes from the Charlotte-Mecklenburg Police Department in North

Carolina. CMPD may not be the first organization you think of when thinking about customer service, but then you have never met Police Chief Johnny Jennings. CMPD's Chief Jennings had a goal. He wanted to make CMPD the Chick-fil-A of policing. He had this epiphany one evening while waiting in the drive-thru of his local Chick-fil-A restaurant. He noticed how not only was the Chick-fil-A team really good at what they did, they also made their customers feel good while they were doing it. Chief Jennings thought, "Why can't we focus on doing this, especially on the 97 percent of calls we receive that do not result in an arrest?"

CMPD created an excellent day in the life of their team members.[4] The video is moving and a reminder to all CMPD team members of what each and every one of their coworkers could be going through. The video opens with a CMPD officer having breakfast with his family before his shift. He is helping his daughter do some last-minute studying for a big test. As he heads out the door for work, a call comes over the radio regarding a carjacking and subsequent search. He is off and running. At the same time, we see a team member handling incoming 911 calls from scared and upset citizens, calming them during their time of trouble, all while receiving a text from an upset child at home. We see a new hire working her first crime scene, and we see a more veteran officer cutting short an argument over finances with her spouse as suspects are apprehended. Each organization that creates a day-in-the-life video can focus on the unique challenges and stresses for their teams, and CMPD gets an A+ for theirs!

If you would like to create your own video, here is how you can start. This exercise is also great if you do not have the time or budget to create an actual video, because it starts the process of building awareness within your teams. Schedule a meeting with departments that work closely together and support one another. If you can get representation from each department, great! If not, get a good mix of longer tenured employees versus new hires. Introduce the concept of a day in the life, stressing the fact that the primary focus is all the stresses, pressure, complaints, and so on that our coworkers are dealing with before interacting with us—things such as job duties, customer demands, deadlines, and quotas.

The video serves as a great reminder—wouldn't this be nice to know before we pick up that phone or respond to that email? We cannot always know, but we can be empathetic to our coworkers that these issues are a common reality.

Break the larger group down into smaller groups (shoot for groups of seven and under—science tells us that collaboration starts to deteriorate once groups are larger than eight). Select your groups strategically—make sure you do not have a group made up of all one department. Make sure each group has a good mix of departments represented.

Then, assign each group an internal customer to focus on, making sure that you have each department in the room represented at least once. The group assignment is this—in 30 minutes, write a day-in-the-life script of the internal customer to which you were assigned. Have the group focus on the stresses, needs, wants, pitfalls—all the things that team member may encounter during the course of an interaction or a day. Here is the fun part—once the groups have drafted their day-in-the-life script, have them act it out as a skit. During each skit, have the other groups in the audience pay close attention to themes that come up during the story. At the end of this exercise, you will have had team members walk in the shoes of each other—and will have the beginning of a script to create a video for your organization.

This session can typically lead to other ideas that continue the focus on internal empathy, such as job shadowing and cross-departmental team-building opportunities.

Note: In our post-pandemic work environments, we often hear that internally focused programs within organizations (such as team-building events, lunch and learns, etc.) were dropped during COVID and have not been brought back. Is this a missing opportunity in your organization right now?

2. Clarify handoffs between departments.

Who owns what? Whose responsibility is it to notify the customer? Whose job is it to set customers' expectations? These are all important questions that too often go unanswered, and our teams are left guessing and making assumptions. The scenario from the patient discharge at Flagler Hospital that was used in the opening of this chapter is a perfect example. In that case, assumptions were being made without any confirmations. The overnight shift nurse would assume the day shift nurse would cover the information. The day shift nurse might assume the doctor would cover the information. Or sometimes maybe the conversation is going to be a difficult one and gets put off and avoided. Regardless of the cause being assumptions or avoidance, the bottom line is if we do not have clear standards set and ownership expectations in place, things will slip through the cracks.

Flagler Hospital knew that changes needed to be made and did something about it. In an initiative led by Donna Wagner, the hospital's vice president and chief nursing officer, the organization examined the current process, identified the gaps and shortcomings, and then created non-negotiable standards for all to follow and be held accountable to.

Alpin Haus is a retailer based in Amsterdam, New York, that specializes in outdoor equipment and services, including camping, skiing, RVs, pools, spas, and more. When company leaders worked on their internal culture, specifically department handoffs, they created training videos showing what a poor customer handoff looks like as well as the proper version. One example focuses on cold transfers. Cold transfers can happen in all businesses if we are not careful. It is when a customer is sent from one employee to another without any or enough information. This can happen on the phone, in person, or electronically. The causes for a cold handoff are several: The department receiving the customer inquiry is just too busy, the inquiry might not be something they can answer ("not my department"), or maybe the customer is angry and the team member just wants to move them along. Most of the time, the reason is much simpler, that warm transfers get missed because the organization never trained the team on what information would be helpful. An easy way to think of warm transfers is one employee sending along any relevant information to the next employee that will help to set them up for success with the customer. Now think about it—how often is that happening in your business? Chances are not often, especially if you have not trained your team to think that way.

3. Understand how your work impacts others. Who does your work support? What group is dependent on your efforts?

Do all your team members know who all their customers are? It is not always obvious; sometimes knowing your customer may take a little work.

Who, really, is your customer?

Ask your employees in every department to define their customer and you will get varying answers. Countless times, when we ask different departments of an organization, "Who is your customer?" we get answers like, "I don't have a customer; I work in the warehouse." It is easy for invisible service providers—those behind the scenes and with little or no external customer contact such as cooks, dishwashers, and factory workers—to think they don't have a customer, and they forget that they can impact the external customer, positively or negatively.

The truth is your primary customer is the person you communicate with directly on a day-to-day basis and who is most affected by the work you do. In the business-to-business world, manufacturing, and corporate office settings, the customer is mostly internal people who work at the same organization. These are positions such as management, administration, IT, HR, marketing, regional sales managers, payroll, branch managers, legal, and regional directors. Every single company we have ever worked with suffers from people in these positions truly not understanding who their customers are, the person/group that is most dependent on their efforts.

Invisible Service Providers

An internal customer relies on the work of an invisible service provider. And, very often, that internal customer may be relying on the invisible service provider to deliver an experience to their external customer. Once you establish who that internal customer is, your internal culture will improve.

> "Everyone in the organization has a customer. It might be the person in the cube next to you or out in the field. It is anyone who is dependent on the job you do."

Sometimes, our team members aren't necessarily aware of their customer. They think that just because they're not in the customer service department or they're not in sales that they don't ultimately serve the customer. However, they also are in customer service. Every team member has some type of impact on the customer experience—but do all your team members know that?

One of the stories we use to illustrate the importance of this knowledge internally at The DiJulius Group is when John was working for UPS part-time while attending college. John would get to work bright and early before class each day to preload UPS trucks so that drivers could then get the packages out. For John, it was a part-time job with hours that fit his schedule well. For the UPS drivers, he played a role that was crucial to their success and overall customer satisfaction. Here is the problem—no one ever told John how important his role was.

Here is a great example of what can happen when we assume what our team members know. John would go in each morning and load the trucks. Trucks were supposed to be loaded in delivery order so the driver could be as efficient as possible. If you would have asked John back then who his customer was, he would have said, "The boxes? I don't have a customer. I load trucks."

John recounts a time when, while loading, he found a small package that should have been loaded on the front right-hand side of the truck for an early delivery. When John located this missing package, the truck was already full, and getting the small box in the absolute correct spot would take quite a bit of work. John decided to toss the box in and get it as close as possible to where it should be. He was a college baseball player after all; he should be able to get it pretty close!

The next morning as John was finishing his shift and the drivers were beginning to stroll in for the start of their shifts, one driver headed straight to John to voice his displeasure. What the driver was upset about was that during his deliveries the previous day, he had found a box in the afternoon that was misloaded. This package was an express delivery that should have been delivered to a location the driver had been to hours earlier. He now had to turn back and wound up with several late packages, many unhappy customers, and got home much later than he should have. All because of John's not-so-accurate toss.

You see, UPS failed to teach John who his customer was—the driver. They failed to teach John a day in the life of a driver and how John's work impacted that driver. Until that moment, John had no idea how important his preloading was. He had no idea that a poor job could lead to several upset customers. He quite simply did not know how great his impact was because no one had ever taken the time to tell him.

> "An employee who works in a support position is like an offensive lineman. The only time their name gets called in a game is when they screw up. The dozens of times they performed well went unnoticed, while everyone else got the recognition."

Think for a moment about your business. Who are your invisible service providers? Do they know who their direct customers are and the impact they can have on them and the external customer? Often they can include departments like IT, HR, the finance team, marketing, and even the cleaning crew.

4. Understand your internal customers.
Get to know other departmental processes.

This focus uses the day-in-the-life-of-a-colleague concept and takes it a step further. Not only do we have to maintain compassion and empathy for our fellow team members, but we also must understand their needs.

Sometimes the culprit is the process itself, or lack of process! Following is a real-life example from Intermountain Health. The health-care industry has something often referred to as the bump list. While it may be called different terms by different organizations, the basic premise is that when a practitioner is no longer available (they call in sick or need a last-minute paid-time-off day), patients need to be rescheduled. This occurrence typically causes several pain points. First, it is a pain point for the medical practitioner's office or clinic, as they will need to help reschedule and perhaps field calls from upset patients. Second, it is a pain point for the organization's contact center, or patient services center, as potentially hundreds of patients will receive notification through the organization's app and then call in looking for information and help. And finally, this is a major pain point for patients, as they now must reschedule an appointment that they may have been waiting for or even dreading!

After the group of roughly 40 team members representing multiple departments of Intermountain Health talked though a typical bump list occurrence, we decided to examine the process. What we found was a bit surprising—there was no official process on what needed to take place when the bump list had to be utilized. Up to this point, different clinics had different strategies. Smaller clinics that saw fewer patients during the day on average dedicated one team member to notify patients. Larger clinics seeing a much larger number of patients could not spare enough people for such a task. What the team realized was that those different processes happening at different clinics were creating some of the chaos that existed. The biggest problem was that the different clinic leaders did not understand the needs of the support center when this occurred. The team focused on creating solutions realized that the organization needed to develop and follow a procedure for dealing with this issue so that the response was consistent, and to help the support team better handle this issue and ultimately assist patients. The team created a new bump list procedure complete with guidelines on when to activate the new process as well as training on how to properly execute the procedure.

What is your "bump list" issue? Every organization has a process somewhere (or lack thereof) that causes chaos and stress internally. Identify one of yours, and create a process that promotes positive change; it is a great start to your internal culture focus.

5. Tighten up communication.

Whenever we are out conducting an internal culture session and ask the question "What are the biggest issues your teams face today?" inevitably the word "communication" comes up. Sometimes it is too much, sometimes it is too little, but communication is always on the top of the list. Most organizations don't take the time to focus on internal communication. It is another area where assumptions are made—that people know how and when to communicate. One place to start when looking to improve internal communication could and should be *negative cues*.

Internal Negative Cues

The exercise of focusing on negative cues is always worthwhile. You will always find something causing confusion or a negative connotation for your customers—both internal and external. Internal negative cues can be more severe because team members do not always view fellow team members as customers—especially if it is not a message being delivered by leadership.

We are all in the customer perception business; no matter what we do, our customer's perception needs to be our reality. To truly understand our customer's perception, we need to view our business through the customer's lens. Obviously, that customer's lens with an internal focus could include someone from sales calling the IT team. Or someone from support receiving an email handoff from sales regarding a new client. When we start this process, we need to remember negative cues happen often without us even knowing. They can hide in the words our teams are using or in the signs that are posted in haste as a reaction to an issue. They could be as simple as a sigh or an eye roll. Many times they are bad habits that have developed over time, and they can "hide" in our blind spots.

Here is an example of a potential verbal negative cue. "You need to verify your information." That is probably something you have heard recently, or it could be something that you say as part of your role.

Now, if we change one word . . . if we change "verify" to "confirm," the tone of this sentence changes . . . just slightly.

Then, if we adjust one more word in the statement—change "you" to "we" so the statement is now "we just need to confirm your information"—now we have taken this statement and changed it from a bit accusatory to advocating for you, all with two small word changes. Think of all the statements your team members are making with each transaction, internal and external, and how many unintentional negative cues may be hiding!

We often hear of internal calls being placed on hold immediately without a greeting; callers being scolded for calling at an inopportune time; or employees not taking the time to respond to internal inquiries versus external inquiries. Perhaps your organization needs to spend some time viewing through the lens of your internal customer?

Other common internal negative cues we see often include habitually being late to meetings or canceling last minute; negative tone of voice in conversations as well as in emails; and inappropriate signage in break rooms or other "back of house" locations. If you would not put it in front of a customer, you should not put it in front of a team member!

Communication Guidelines

The next step that companies with amazing internal cultures take is to create standards and guidelines for communication. When the team at Alpin Haus in Upstate New York got together to focus on standards, they created a comprehensive list of non-negotiable standards for internal communication. The team, led by company CEO Andy Heck and VP of marketing and CXO, Katie Osborn, realized many issues that negatively affected customers were 100 percent avoidable with a sharper focus on internal communication habits. One new rule is no more assumptions being made after reading vague messages. The organization employs standards that all team members are trained on and then are accountable to execute. (See Image 7.1.)

INTERNAL COMMUNICATION BEST PRACTICES

Image 7.1

Email is probably one of the biggest culprits when it comes to communication issues. What happens with emails in your organization right now? Are there standards in place for your team to follow, or is it the Wild West? Busch Funeral Homes did a deep dive into their internal culture, which included some folks with very long tenure with the organization. Based in Ohio, Busch Funeral Homes is family-owned and -operated, serving families in Cleveland and surrounding communities for over 100 years. The team at Busch realized there were several inconsistencies in their teams' use of email and decided it was time to create some standards. As you read through Busch's email best practices in Image 7.2, you may be thinking that many items are common sense. We must remember: Common sense is not always that common. Then ask yourself how many of the "email nevers" happen in your organization right now. Chances are, a lot!

IMAGE 7.2: BUSCH WORLD-CLASS INTERNAL CULTURE

Email Best Practices	The Four Reasons to Email Internally
Ensuring our external customer's emails are the most important things in our inbox	1. Officially communicate a question/decision 2. Confirm or schedule appointments 3. Document important conversations 4. Send Busch or team announcements

Email Never	Email Always
• Take more than three emails to discuss something • Communicate daily or weekly needs • Send to unnecessary groups or addresses • "Reply all" to save time • Place someone in "TO:" that doesn't require reply • Email researchers about urgent matters • Ignore or put off a reply • Reply with an uncertainty of your next action • Complain, reprimand, or argue • Send unnecessary emails after hours • (7pm–7am) or when someone is on vacation	• Use phone or Teams for detailed discussions • Use QS or Huddle to share daily or weekly needs • Send to the minimum amount of addresses • "Reply all" only if all need details • Use "cc:" to include those who don't need to reply • Call, then email, with researchers and urgent matters • Respond promptly • Reply with a clear commitment and deadline "Got it" • Personally communicate • Consider work-life balance

6. Create and improve training.

On the surface, training sounds easy. We created all these great new standards and had them printed out on nice posterboard . . . of course everyone will want to be on board! The reality is training is the hardest part of any initiative. We need to make sure that all the content we have created is available for our team members and they know they are accountable to know and execute on the standards. We need to know that all team members are trained on the material and that these are topics being discussed regularly in department meetings and huddles. This is not something you can create and then hope it catches on after one meeting. Focus and effort are required. And our leaders need to be leading by example.

That is why the following example from Excite Credit Union really stands out. The Excite team, led by CEO Brian Dorcy and CXO Richard Walter, knew that the success of their external and internal experience initiatives lay with departmental directors and managers. That is why they created the reminder (Image 7.3) for their leaders as part of this focus.

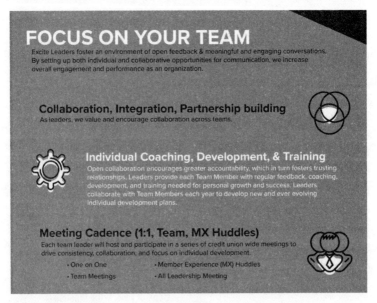

Image 7.3

Are you spending enough time experiencing
your own customer experience?

With overall customer satisfaction in all industries dropping to 20-year lows,[5] more and more CEOs have decided to literally get on the front lines to better educate themselves on what it is really like to be their customer and customer-facing employees.

Uber CEO Dara Khosrowshahi and Lyft CEO David Risher are spending time shuttling passengers. New Starbucks CEO Laxman Narasimhan is working as a barista each month. In 2022, DoorDash started requiring every employee—from engineers to CEO—to make food deliveries once a month. Khosrowshahi told the *Wall Street Journal* that his experience moonlighting as an Uber driver led him to "reevaluate every single assumption that we've made."[6]

According to a Pew Research Center survey, low pay, few opportunities for advancement, and disrespect on the job were the top reasons workers cited for quitting.[7] For these reasons alone it is critical that senior leaders as well as anyone who works at corporate headquarters—those who are removed from the day-to-day operations of the company—spend adequate time working alongside customer-facing employees. It is an incredible learning experience to better understand what a day in the life of both your customers and employees looks like, and see firsthand the frustration, pain points, and bottlenecks both customers and your employees are dealing with. Unless you have executive sponsorship (aka buy-in), nothing will change. Having executives working on the front lines often leads to changes that improve both the customer and employee experience.

According to a survey from e-learning and HR publishing platform eLearning Industry, a majority (53 percent) of employees feel their bosses are out of touch with what they need and want.[8] Not a shock when you learn that CEOs spend only 6 percent of their time with frontline employees on average.[9] Who knows better what customers want—a person who spends 6 percent of their time with the customer or an employee who spends 100 percent of their time? Spending time in customer-facing roles as a senior leader is no longer a luxury. It is vital to improving your customer experience and reducing employee turnover. When a CEO is present and willing to be in the trenches with their customer-facing employees, sleeves rolled up, elbow to elbow, it goes a long way with employee engagement and retention.

Airbnb's CEO Spent Six Months Living in His Company's Rentals—and Found the Core Problem

"To make a change, you have to touch the product, the policies, the service across all these different touch points," says Brian Chesky, CEO of Airbnb. Chesky spent six months as a host and guest of his own business. "Last year, I started living in Airbnbs, and I stayed in like a dozen and a half over the course of six months," Chesky told *Fortune*. He continued staying exclusively in Airbnbs for a year as the "ultimate guest" and started noticing how much the quality of the homes and experiences varied.

"You always want to work on something new, but when you have a service like ours, and so many people use it, it's easy to forget what they actually want. You have to have their permission to do new things," Chesky says. "A good lesson is: Fall back in love with your core business." His embracing of the "nitty-gritty" meant making improvements while doing the less glamorous work; in his words, "being a glorified customer support agent."[10]

8

BUILDING AND DEVELOPING GREAT LEADERS

*"When your company says you want your employees
to be leaders, what that really means is that you
want their emotional commitment to your vision. A
leader's emotional commitment is about taking on
the company success as a personal crusade."*

—STAN SLAP, GROWTH GURU

Do You Have Accidental Bosses?

An article in Fortune titled "Nearly all bosses are 'accidental' with
no formal training—and research shows it's leading 1 in 3 workers
to quit" shares research conducted by the Chartered Management
Institute revealing that many of those promoted into managerial
positions are all title and no training.[1] These startling findings
revealed one in four people in the workforce have management
responsibilities, yet very few have been trained to do their jobs.

CMI's research found that an incredible 82 percent of bosses
are "accidental managers," and what's even scarier is 25 percent

of those are in senior leadership roles. This is negatively impacting employee morale and a third of employees are quitting their jobs.

Employees who say their manager is ineffective feel seriously less satisfied, valued, and motivated in their job than those who described their managers as effective. Fifty percent of employees surveyed who are unhappy with their manager say they are planning to quit within the next year.

Employees are not the only ones with low morale. Many of these accidental managers were high-performing employees prior to being promoted without any leadership training. According to CMI's research, managers aren't confident in their own leadership abilities, with many struggling when it comes to dealing with the multiple issues facing their team members at work and in their home lives.

When entrepreneurs start a company, they find a few crazy people to join them, people who see how their vision will change the world. That founding group of employees rallies together, makes ridiculous sacrifices, fails, innovates, fails some more, and eventually figures it out. Why? Because the founding team members were in the foxhole with the entrepreneur. It was "them against the world." After they get through that phase, growth comes, and more employees are needed, resulting in layers of leadership, and now you have employees being hired by people who don't have that fuel and emotional connection to the original rebels. You lose your mavericks, and the soul of a start-up disappears. The magic that was a magnetic force attracting rock stars who would follow the founder into battle is gone. Now it is about growth and hitting our numbers, productivity, and efficiency.

An infinitely better alternative: building and developing great leaders. The key is to replicate that entrepreneurial spirit, instilling it into the next generations of leaders who will rally their teams around the company's cause. This is much easier said than done. But if your leaders are not infused with that energy, your employees never will be.

Building a great internal culture and leading the Employee Experience Revolution starts with developing great leaders, making your existing ones better, and creating a pipeline of emerging talent who can be the next generation of great leaders in your company.

Leadership Burnout

The Great Resignation wasn't only about turnover at the employee level. Leaders at all levels quit and moved on for the same reasons employees quit, including burnout and lack of respect, meaning, and purpose in their careers. And just like the hasty way in which organizations replaced employee turnover, companies compromised when replacing their leaders and/or rushed the process, setting up their emerging leaders for failure and additional stress.

Leaders at every level bore the brunt of turnover and attrition fallout, especially middle managers. When a team member quits, it is almost always the leaders' responsibility to pick up the pieces. Rehires don't happen overnight. Shifts need to be covered, an attempt needs to be made at keeping up morale among employees who have chosen to stay, and interviewing, training replacements, and dealing with customer complaints that inevitably come with newer customer-facing employees all have to get done.

Over the last few years, we have asked more of our leaders than ever before. Let's reward them, let's help them, let's support, train, and inspire them. To retain existing leaders and attract future leaders, let's make leadership something that people once again aspire to.

Identifying Your Emerging Leaders

Emerging leaders are team members who not only perform their jobs well, but also demonstrate potential for growth and leadership beyond their current roles, primarily by demonstrating emotional intelligence. They are also willing to take on challenges and are proactive in seeking solutions. They demonstrate a natural ability to inspire their colleagues. Following are some specifics to look for in your high performers:

QUALITIES FOR IDENTIFYING EMERGING LEADERS

- Overall job performance: This one is obvious but often given too much weight in identifying a future leader. Future leaders can stand out due to consistency and results. But this is not the only measure to use.

- Showing leadership tendencies: Even while being a member of the team, leaders of the future may show leadership qualities such as supporting fellow team members, taking the lead on projects, or superior problem solving.

- Innovation: Future leaders do not subscribe to the "we've always done it this way" mentality and are not afraid to propose new solutions. Thanks to their focus on problem-solving, they often find new and more efficient ways to do things.

- Adaptability: Adapting to change is critical in today's business landscape. Future leaders are the ones who embrace change and look for new opportunities to grow and learn.

- Communication: Effective communication is key to strong leadership. Your future leaders will not only demonstrate the ability to communicate clearly, but also, and maybe most importantly, the ability to listen actively and take direction.

- Collaboration: Leaders understand the value of teamwork and collaboration. Your future leaders will be those individuals who contribute positively to group dynamics and support their colleagues.

- Ownership: Emerging leaders take ownership of their roles and responsibilities, going above and beyond what is expected. They proactively seek opportunities to make a difference and don't wait for directions. Recognizing those who show initiative and responsibility can lead to the discovery of potential leaders.

Once an emerging leader has been identified, what are the next steps to take for continued development? Find ways to get them active within the organization outside of just their current role. One good way is to invite them to join a project steering committee where they can interact with leaders, oversee timelines, and communicate progress.

Develop Leaders to Be Human First

New and existing leaders tend to focus heavily on results. Why? Because all their incentives are tied to results. Too many leaders had poor role models early on in their careers. The managers they worked for led by fear and intimidation, focusing only on productivity and top- and bottom-line results, often at the expense of the teams they managed. Leaders need to strike a balance between getting results and being understanding and empathetic with employees to get their buy-in emotionally and physically. And while it can be difficult to plan and focus on leadership training when many are in a hiring crisis, the reality is the time is now for organizations to focus on developing great leaders. It is never too early to start preparing someone for leadership.

The single most important determinant of a person's performance and commitment to stay with an organization is the relationship a person has with their immediate manager. As stated in McKinsey & Company's article, "The Boss Factor: Making the World a Better Place Through Workplace Relationships," improving a worker's job satisfaction can be the most important thing a leader can do. "Few managers realize what a dramatic impact— either positive or negative—they have on the world through their everyday behavior. It is the responsibility of senior leaders to enlighten them and provide the organizational context that consistently fosters high-quality relationships between bosses and the people who report to them."[2]

In the digital revolution, human interaction, compassion, empathy, and communication skills become a premium advantage. It's time to consider an entirely different approach: building human-centric employee experiences through genuinely caring about your people. So, get to know your employees, humanize them, humanize yourself.

> **"Care before coach."**
> **—Ken Blanchard, author**

Two New Skill Sets No Leader Needed until Now

We live in a different world today ever since the COVID-19 pandemic; on top of everything else we have always expected from our leaders, now there are two new leadership skills no one prior was required to possess. These have never been taught in any business school or leadership development course. Today's leaders now need to know how to 1) lead from a distance and 2) recognize and support employees' mental well-being.

Recognize and Support Employees' Mental Well-Being

Talk about a paradigm shift. Leaders today need to be aware of the direct and indirect costs when employees don't have the emotional and psychological support they need. Both topics are discussed in greater detail in chapter 6.

Stop Policing and Start Leading

At most companies, policies and processes are put in place to deal with employees who exhibit sloppy, unprofessional, or irresponsible behavior. If you avoid or move these people out, you don't need so many rules. If you build an organization made up of high performers, you can eliminate most controls. The denser the talent, the greater the freedom you can offer.

In his book *No Rules Rules*, cofounder of Netflix Reed Hastings shares how in his first business, Pure Software, he found out the hard way about having too much structure and too many policies. "Policies and control processes became so foundational to our work that those who were great at coloring within the lines were promoted, while many creative mavericks felt stifled and went to work elsewhere. Then two things occurred. The first is that we failed to innovate quickly. We had become increasingly efficient and decreasingly creative." Hastings points out that as industries shift, most firms fail to adapt. "To survive, we needed

184 The Employee Experience Revolution

to change. But we had selected and conditioned our employees to follow a process, not to think freshly or shift fast."[3]

Behind Every Successful Person Is a Long List of Failures

"With my next company, Netflix, I hoped to promote flexibility, employee freedom, and innovation, instead of error prevention and rule adherence. At the same time, I understood that as a company grows, if you don't manage it with policies or control processes, the organization is likely to descend into chaos," explains Hastings. "If you give employees more freedom instead of developing processes to prevent them from exercising their own judgment, they will make better decisions and it's easier to hold them accountable."[4]

Businesses need to stop treating their employees like children. Leadership needs to be about helping people reach their potential in performance, not managing them away from breaking policy or screwing up. Employee experience is a critical factor for current employees and job seekers alike. High performers need innovation; innovators need autonomy. Don't let one poor employee ruin your organization's freedom and flexibility. Process kills organizational flexibility. Fear kills creativity and innovation. Employee freedom means they can take a lot of risks and sometimes fail. Risk-taking breeds innovation.

> **"Don't punish 98 percent of your team members because you are afraid what 2 percent will do."**

Jeff Bezos Encourages His Leaders to Fail. Often.

"One of my jobs as the leader of Amazon is to encourage people to be bold. And people love to focus on things that aren't yet working and that's good. It's human nature; that kind of divine discontent can be very helpful," Jeff Bezos, Amazon's founder, shares in an interview with *Business Insider*. "But it's incredibly hard to get people to take bold bets. And you need to encourage that." He acknowledges that these bold bets will be experiments with potential for big success or epic failure, and more likely the latter. Still, he knows that several big successes make up for numerous ideas that ultimately go nowhere. "So bold bets: AWS, Kindle, Amazon Prime, our third-party seller business, all of those things are examples of bold bets that did work, and they paid for a lot of experiments."[5]

Bezos stresses that what really matters are the consequences of companies being too afraid to experiment, even if it means they sometimes fail. "They eventually get in a desperate position where the only thing they can do is a kind of Hail Mary bet at the very end of their corporate existence."[6]

> "I would rather reward spectacular failures than mediocre accomplishments."
> —Tom Peters, author

There Are No Bad Teams, Only Bad Leaders

There is a great story in the book *Extreme Ownership* by Jocko Willink and Leif Babin. During a Navy SEALs BUDs training, SEAL candidates were grouped into boat crews of seven men and assigned to an inflatable boat that weighed more than 200 pounds. The most senior-ranking candidate became the boat-crew leader responsible for receiving, transmitting, and overseeing the execution of the lead instructor's orders. They went through a grueling string of races that involved running with the boat and then paddling it in the ocean.

After several rounds, one specific team consistently came in first and one specific team consistently came in last every time. The instructors decided to switch the leaders of the best and worst teams, and the results were remarkable. Under their new leader, the performance of the team that was originally winning all the events went down, and they finished in the middle of the pack. The team that previously was finishing last now started winning every race with their new leader.

The once-great team could not overcome a bad leader, who was unable to command respect or maintain synchronicity. Meanwhile, the excellent leader had taken his new team from last to first by getting them to believe that they were just as capable as his former team, and that bickering with each other during the exercise would not be tolerated.[7]

Employee Experience Revolutionary Leaders

The primary question great companies need to focus on when building a world-class internal culture is "How does a leader help their employees live an extraordinary life?" Research shows that this type of leadership mentality enhances both team performance and satisfaction.

Studies demonstrate that managers themselves are happier and find their roles more meaningful when customers are happier, employees are happier, and when they feel they are helping their team members.[8]

However, leaders will struggle with fully embracing this type of leadership style until senior management stops incentivizing the wrong behaviors and instead provides the necessary leadership soft skills training that results in higher employee satisfaction. Gallup research contends that only one in ten people possesses the necessary traits that great managers exhibit, traits that include building relationships that create trust, open dialogue, and transparency.[9]

In a *Harvard Business Review* article, "Why Do So Many Incompetent Men Become Leaders?" organizational psychologist Tomas Chamorro-Premuzic suggests that many leaders achieve their positions by being self-centered, overconfident, narcissistic, arrogant, manipulative, and risk-prone.[10] While this may still be true in many organizations, the times of uncaring, fear-based leadership are coming to an end. It is when employees feel their leaders are approachable and truly care about them as human beings that the strongest organizations are built. Leaders enjoying their own roles more takes this training and management approach full circle.

The Power of Storytelling:
Why Leaders Must Be Great Storytellers

Storytelling is a powerful tool used for centuries to convey important messages and lessons. Stories can capture people's attention, engage their emotions, and inspire action. In recent years, storytelling has become increasingly important in the workplace as leaders have recognized its potential to motivate employees, build strong teams, and drive business results. In addition to other leadership skills, leaders must be great storytellers.

Storytelling has been shown to activate different parts of the brain than traditional communication methods like facts and figures. When we hear a story, our brains release dopamine, a chemical that helps us feel pleasure and motivation. This chemical response makes us more receptive to information and more likely to remember it. Additionally, stories can help us connect emotionally to a message, which can increase its impact and influence. You may have heard the old saying "Data tells, stories sell!" A great story helps to make that connection with the audience—in this case, a leader's team.

A study conducted by neuroscientist Paul Zak found that stories following a narrative arc with a beginning, middle, and end, and including emotional elements, can increase oxytocin levels in the brain.[11] Oxytocin is a hormone associated with increased trust, empathy, and cooperation. This means that when leaders use storytelling in the workplace, they can increase their employees' levels of oxytocin, making them more likely to trust each other and work together effectively. Science shows that storytelling is a powerful leadership tool.

Because of this oxytocin release, stories can be used in the workplace to inspire, motivate, and engage employees. They can help employees understand the company's values and mission and provide context for decisions that may be difficult to understand. Additionally, stories can be used to create a sense of community and teamwork among employees, as they can share stories that illustrate their shared experiences and goals.

The Role of Leaders in Storytelling

Leaders play a critical storytelling role in the workplace. They are responsible for communicating the company's vision and goals to employees, and for inspiring and motivating them to achieve those goals. Additionally, the art of leadership storytelling can be used to build relationships with employees while creating a culture in which team members feel fully informed and free to ask questions and share ideas of their own.

Research from a study conducted by the Center for Creative Leadership found that effective storytelling by leaders can increase engagement, commitment, and performance among employees. When leaders use storytelling to communicate their own personal experiences and connect with their employees on an emotional level, they can build stronger relationships and create a more positive workplace culture.[12]

Storytelling has the power to inspire, motivate, and engage employees in the workplace, to help them see beyond the status quo. Leaders who are skilled storytellers can use this tool to drive business results, build strong teams, and create a culture of openness and transparency. By understanding the science of storytelling, the importance of storytelling in the workplace, and the role of leaders in storytelling, leaders can use this tool to create a more engaged and productive workforce, becoming more effective leaders in the process and ultimately having a major impact on the customer's experience.

How do we get leaders to become great storytellers?

First, our leaders must understand the overall importance of storytelling. Before diving into the training process, it's crucial to emphasize the significance of storytelling in a leader's role. Stories have been an integral part of human communication for centuries, as they engage both the rational and emotional aspects of the brain. A well-told story can ignite passion, build trust, and foster a sense of purpose among team members, ultimately leading to higher productivity and improved team dynamics.

Second on the list is training leaders on the key components of telling a compelling story. The four main components of a story are:

1. Purpose

Every story needs a clear and concise purpose, whether it is to motivate the team, illustrate a point, or share a valuable lesson. Leaders must align the story with the intended message to ensure coherence. They need to know the purpose first and draft the story accordingly. A nice story cannot simply be told with the hopes of having a purpose somewhere; the purpose of each story must be resolute.

2. Emotional Connection

Great stories evoke emotions. Leaders should learn how to connect with their audience by applying authentic reflection: incorporating emotions such as empathy, inspiration, or humor into their narratives. Focus on stories that team members can relate to, which include situations they may find themselves in from time to time. Reach out to them on a human level within the business context. Find and share stories of a team member overcoming conflict or barriers to achieve success. Work in "inside jokes" of the department to build humor and camaraderie.

3. Structure

If not focused and prepared, it is easy to take a great theme and turn it into a ramble. An effective story typically follows a structure, including an introduction, a conflict or challenge, a climax, and a resolution. When leaders focus on structuring their narratives, they maintain engagement and interest, avoiding wordiness and rabbit holes.

4. Authenticity

Authenticity is key to building trust. To create genuine connections with their team members, leaders should be encouraged to share purposeful leadership stories including personal experiences and insights. These can come from stories of their own growth within the organization, a department, or a specific position. They are not "back in my day" type of lessons, but more focused on situations where the storyteller grew and learned as a result, ultimately attaining their leadership role.

Another key aspect of creating great storytellers in your organization is leveraging technology. Incorporating technology into storytelling can enhance effectiveness and engagement. But you must be careful! Technology should only be used to enhance the story; it should not become the story. What this means is that the story does not get listed out in bullet-point fashion as a reminder to the storyteller—or "death by PowerPoint" as it has been called. But, if a picture can be added to help take the audience to the place and time, that is a great thing.

Encouraging Continuous Improvement

Becoming a skilled storyteller requires practice and continuous improvement of one's communication skills. Leaders should be encouraged to seek feedback coaching from their peers, superiors, and even team members. Organizations should also look for opportunities for further development, including meeting for peer group practice sessions, offering classes, or starting a Toastmasters or other speaking club.

Storytelling is a powerful and effective leadership skill that can transform senior-level employees into influential and empathetic leaders. Through purposeful training, practice, and embracing technology, leaders can learn to craft compelling stories that inspire, engage, and create a lasting impact within their teams and organizations. Embracing the art of storytelling will undoubtedly elevate leaders' communication and foster a more cohesive and motivated workforce, ultimately leading to the overarching goal of a best-in-class customer experience.

For successful leadership experience—as well as the highest-level employee experience—storytelling should become an integral part of your organization's upskilling strategy!

Being a Leader in the Relationship Economy

In John's book, *The Relationship Economy: Building Stronger Customer Connections in the Digital Age*, he focuses on how today the primary currency is made up of the connections and trust among customers, employees, and vendors that create significantly more value in what we sell (to our customers) and pay (to our employees).

Today we are living in the digital disruption era. Technology has provided us with unprecedented advances, information, knowledge, instant access, and entertainment. We have computers, mobile phones, tablets, the internet, social media, apps, and artificial intelligence. However, as convenient as these advances have made our lives, they have come at a significant cost. They have changed the way we communicate, behave, and think and have led to a dramatic decline in our people skills in every generation. As a society we are now relationship disadvantaged. We no longer become curious about others or eager to engage in conversations. The younger generation, at no fault of their own, primarily communicates electronically, and the explosion of ecommerce means we go out less and less. In business, multichannel communication has dramatically reduced phone calls to companies; customers can get answers via chatbots and self-service kiosks, and place orders via email, websites, or through social media channels. All are valuable alternatives, but they come with unintended consequences.

Act as if Today Is the Day You Will Be Remembered for How You Treat Others

The single biggest factor contributing to where you are today remains the relationships you have acquired over your lifetime. The people in your life have significantly impacted your professional and personal success, happiness, and accomplishments and vice versa. That will be true ten and 20 years from now. It will be true when you are on your deathbed reflecting on the life you have lived.

Everyone we meet has an invisible sign above their head that reads:

"MAKE ME FEEL IMPORTANT!"

It is human nature to be preoccupied with what is happening in our world. However, to build a connection with another person, we need to put our focus on them, particularly on making that person feel better for having interacted with us or chosen to work for us. When we are totally present with someone, focused on them, that's when the magic happens.

We couldn't agree more with the following statement by Stephen Covey:

> "People don't listen with the intent of understanding; they listen with the intent of replying."

Scientists have studied the human brain and found it takes a minimum of 0.6 seconds to formulate a response to something said. Then they researched hundreds of conversations and found the average gap between people talking was 0.2 seconds.[13] How is it that people can respond in a third of the time that the human brain allows? Obviously people have their responses ready long before the other person has finished talking.

How does this translate to our professional life? As leaders we need to focus on team members and building an emotional connection with each of them. To prove that you are focusing on learning more about your employees, you need to focus on knowing two or more facts about their FORD, as discussed in previous chapters.

Following are some examples of the type of information you can casually collect about FORD.

Family

For most people, this is the hottest button of all. Are they married? How long have they been married? What is the name of their significant other? Do they have kids? How old are their kids? What activities are their kids into? Where was their most recent family trip?

Occupation

This one is easy; they work for you. However, do you know what their last job was? What was their title? What is their degree in? How did they get into this industry? What made them come to your company?

Recreation

This is what people geek out about. What are their hobbies? What do they do for fun, with their free time? What do they do for exercise—running, lifting, yoga, and so on? Do they have a favorite team, sport, college?

Dreams

What are their long-term goals? What do they see themselves doing in five years? Where are they dying to travel? What is on their bucket list?

If you can find out about two of these subjects, you not only have a relationship, you *own* that relationship. FORD represents people's hot buttons, what each individual cares about the most. FORD is what they are passionate about. It is the topics that make them light up, that they talk about in detail. Constantly referring to their FORD keeps the focus of the conversation on the other person.

Every time you communicate with a team member, you should be collecting and utilizing FORD. It is extremely simple to work in a few questions about these subjects in the natural flow of a conversation. We have been intentionally practicing the FORD technique in every conversation for more than a decade, and no one has ever said to either of us, "You sure ask a lot of questions." It is quite the opposite. Once you get someone talking, typically they will end up offering most of the information all on their own. All you have to do is sit back and listen.

> **"Today's illiterates are those who have an inability to make meaningful connections with others."**

Digital Intelligence Up, Emotional Intelligence Down

Due to the digital revolution, many leaders lack the necessary people skills of previous generations. Yet they are now leading start-ups that have developed quickly into leading companies. This will only accelerate the growing number of relationship-disadvantaged businesses.

In a TED Talk, hospitality entrepreneur Chip Conley addressed this phenomenon. "He [Conley] realized he could become what he calls a 'Modern Elder,' someone with the 'ability to use timeless wisdom and apply it to modern-day problems.' For instance, he shares with the younger employees the people skills he gained over decades, while they teach him about technology. Nearly 40 percent of Americans have a boss who is younger than them—and when people of all ages exchange knowledge and learn from each other, good things happen. 'This is the new sharing economy,' Conley says."[14]

A 2010 study by the Relational Capital Group revealed that 89 percent of senior leaders believe that relationships are the most important factor in their success year over year. However, the study also revealed that only 24 percent of these leaders actually do anything intentionally to promote building those relationships. Finally, the study further indicated that less than 5 percent of organizations actually have any specific strategies for helping their professionals develop and strengthen the relationships required to achieve their goals.[15]

What It Takes to Master Rapport Building in Leadership

No one is born with a rapport-building gene. And not everyone is inclined to be outgoing or to strike up a conversation with people they don't know. The environment you grow up in plays a big part in how you act. If you had extremely outgoing parents, chances are you will grow up to behave similarly. However, even if you were not exposed to an outgoing environment in your early years, this skill set can certainly be developed and mastered. There are certain sets of characteristics you need to work on to master relationship building. To develop strong relationships you:

1. Must love people

2. Must be authentic

3. Must have incredible empathy

4. Must be obsessively curious

5. Must be a great listener

1. Must Love People

If you do not genuinely love people, you don't belong or deserve to be leading anyone. John has never hesitated to say, "I love my employees. They believe in me, my vision, and have dedicated their careers to helping me achieve that. They don't owe me, I owe them." Great leadership is largely a matter of love. It involves genuinely caring for and loving your employees and your customers. To really serve people you must love people.

Author Fred Reichheld says, "Love is the state of caring so much for a person that most of your own happiness derives from increasing that person's happiness and well-being."[16] To John, that is ultimately what leadership is about.

2. Must Be Authentic

People have great BS detectors. Your interest in others and your desire to make a connection must be authentic. If you are asking questions merely for appearances or just to get them to do what you say, people will see through you. Not being authentic will earn you a poor reputation. You are much better off simply coming out and asking for what you want; people will respect you more. Instead of trying to manipulate people, you must show them you care. You need to demonstrate that you are genuinely interested in others and that you realize they are human beings with lives and not just employees you are trying to make more productive.

3. Must Have Incredible Empathy

One of our strongest human talents is the ability to empathize with another person's situation. Seeing and understanding someone's experience from their perspective, walking in their shoes, is key.

A LEADER'S SUPERPOWER

We spend much of our time trying to understand what our customers, employees, significant others, and children really mean by what they say or don't say. Too often we try to analyze, decode, or judge without ever knowing what is going on.

"Empathy is a real-life human superpower," says Dr. Ali Hill, sociologist and emotional intelligence evangelist. "When we truly empathize with others, we come as close to reading minds as humans can get. When we turn off our analysis mechanisms and instead just listen and attempt to think from the other person's point of view, the message becomes much clearer. When we empathize, we can actually feel what the other person is feeling. And when we can feel what someone else feels, then we inherently understand what they're trying to communicate. Pretty powerful stuff, empathy."[17]

Empathy is especially effective when paired with compassion. Compassion is the desire to help another person. Together empathy and compassion are the two most powerful soft skills leaders can have. When you genuinely serve with compassion and empathy, your leadership rises to a completely different level. The challenge for most companies is how to teach these skills to their leaders and employees. How do you make them more than mere buzzwords and platitudes? The answer is by having your leaders constantly putting themselves in the shoes of the employee. When you truly understand the employees' plight, what they're going through, the importance of each interaction becomes crystal clear. (See "day in the life of an employee" in chapter 7, under the "Remove silos" section.)

The ability to see things from the perspective of others is key to making a connection, building a relationship, and achieving overall business success. It allows you to explore other people's viewpoints and the possibility that your own opinion may be incorrect. Having empathy, experts say, improves your leadership, teaches you to ask the right questions, boosts teamwork, and allows you to understand your customers.[18] It is a powerful gift.

Forging strong relationships relies on all these skills—being interested in someone else's life, truly listening, and practicing empathy and compassion. They're the building blocks of becoming a great leader. Leaders who speak last can create a more collaborative and inclusive environment, one that fosters open communication, encourages diverse perspectives, and leads to better decision-making overall.

4. Must Be Obsessively Curious

Those who are the strongest at relationship building are extremely curious. They are dying to learn about others and their experiences. They are curious not only about subjects that interest them but also about unfamiliar subjects. They become investigative reporters, wanting to learn as much as possible about other people's lives and passions. They truly enjoy learning; they explore what makes human beings tick.

BE CURIOUS, NOT JUDGMENTAL

One of the most recent popular TV series is *Ted Lasso*, played by Jason Sudeikis. If you haven't ever seen it, go watch it today. In contrast to all the negative, doom and gloom shows out there, *Ted Lasso* is inspiring, funny, and entertaining. Most of all, he makes you want to be a better person. There is a great clip from the show where Ted is sandbagging the villainous, arrogant, billionaire soccer team owner, Rupert, in a game of darts.

> You know, Rupert, guys have underestimated me my entire life. And for years, I never understood why. It used to really bother me. But then one day, I was driving my little boy to school, and I saw this quote by Walt Whitman, and it was painted on the wall there. It said, "Be curious, not judgmental." I like that.
>
> So, I get back in my car and I'm driving to work, and all of a sudden it hits me. All them fellas that used to belittle me, not a single one of them were curious. You know, they thought they had everything all figured out. So, they judged everything, and they judged everyone. And I realized that their underestimating me . . . who I was had nothing to do with it. 'Cause if they were curious, they would've asked questions. You know? Like, "Have you played a lot of darts, Ted?"
>
> To which I would've answered, "Yes, sir. Every Sunday afternoon at a sports bar with my father, from age ten until I was 16 when he passed away."[19]

Those who are the strongest at relationship building are extremely curious. They are eager to learn about others and their experiences. They are curious not only about subjects that interest them but also about unfamiliar subjects. They truly enjoy learning; they explore what makes human beings tick.

The best relationship builders appear like detectives in their conversations, looking for clues to finding out what makes the other person unique and memorable. They're after things you won't find on their Facebook page or LinkedIn profile. "Highly empathic people have an insatiable curiosity about strangers," said Roman Krznaric, author of *Empathy: Why It Matters, and How to Get It.* "They will talk to the person sitting next to them on the bus."[20]

Such curiosity leads to empathy expanding quite naturally during interactions with those outside our usual crowd, people who tend to view the world at least somewhat differently than we do.

The authors of the book *Superconnector* explain how great connectors operate: "Connectors have small talk with a purpose. They are never just engaging in conversation for the sake of conversation."[21] There is always a goal of gleaning from the other person the most pertinent information about them at the core level, for potential future reference.

5. Must Be a Great Listener

There is a lot more to being a good listener than just letting the other person talk. You need to be attentive, patient, make good eye contact, not interrupt, ask probing questions, and finally pause to process what you heard before responding.

How can you perfect the art of listening? Ask fascinating, probing questions, follow-up questions, and even more questions. Then be silent and let the person speak their piece. You learn valuable insights not from asking one question, but through an unstructured back-and-forth dialogue. As Tom Peters notes in his book *The Excellence Dividend*, "If you ask a question and don't ask two or three follow-up questions, odds are you weren't listening to the answer. A good listener becomes INVISIBLE; makes the respondent the centerpiece."[22]

FIERCE ATTENTION

Peters dedicates an entire chapter to listening in which he writes, "Attention is one thing. FIERCE attention resides on a different planet."[23] He believes fierce attention is of such high degree that the person responding to you feels totally engrossed and as if the focus is completely on them. And rather than merely listening or improving your listening skills, Peters believes in making fierce listening your number one strategic goal, the primary trait differentiating you from everyone else.

Fierce attention means, if you ask a question and don't ask two to three follow-up (clarifying) questions, odds are you weren't listening, or you just asked the question to be polite, as in, "How was your weekend?" or you were dying to answer it yourself. When talking to others, we should aim for a 4:1 ratio of questions asked versus answered.

It is not about listening so you can decide when to chime in with your own opinion; it is about listening to actually understand. Asking these two questions can dramatically help anyone's ability to listen to understand: "Can you tell me more?" and "Can you help me better understand?"

THE ART OF LISTENING

"Listening to understand is often the only way of showing people they are special and that you care for them," says Rich Simmonds in his blog post "The Art of Listening . . . Leading and Selling". He adds, "If you are unable to connect with people to the point that they can trust you, they will not follow you as a leader or give you the opportunity to serve them as a leader. These are the basics of a relationship, and trust will only be sustainable in the safety of a relationship."

Without listening with the goal of understanding, we don't learn about others' insecurities or, for that matter, our own. And insecurities are something we all have in common. As Simmonds also points out, "It is our task to show people we care, not so that we can blatantly manipulate them into using our product or service, but rather by listening and trying to understand them where they are."[24] Empathetic listening will help us determine what people really need so we can provide it in a way that is tailored specifically for them, resulting in a situation where everyone wins.

MYTHS OF A GOOD LISTENER

In their *Harvard Business Review* article "What Great Listeners Actually Do," authors Jack Zenger and Joseph Folkman explain how most people believe they are better-than-average listeners. They reveal the myth of how people believe good listening comes down to:

1. Remaining silent while others are speaking.

2. Using facial expressions and verbal sounds ("*mmm-hmm*") to indicate that you're listening to others.

3. Repeating word for word what others said. We have all been taught this practice and heard the following comment: "So, let me make sure I understand you. What you're saying is . . ."[25]

Research suggests that these behaviors fall far short of superior listening skills. The article cites a study comparing the best listeners to average listeners and identifying the characteristics that make an outstanding listener:

- **Good listening is much more than being silent.** It is actually the opposite; people perceive the best listeners to be those who periodically ask questions that stimulate further discovery and insight. Sitting silently nodding does not provide sure evidence that a person is listening. Good listening is consistently seen as a two-way dialogue. The best conversations are active.

- **Good listening includes interactions that build a person's self-esteem.** The best listeners make the conversation a positive experience for the other party, which doesn't happen when the listener is passive. Good listeners make the other person feel supported and convey confidence in them.

- **Good listening is seen as a cooperative conversation.** In these interactions, feedback flows smoothly in both directions with neither party becoming defensive about comments the other made. By contrast, poor listeners are seen as competitive—as listening only to identify errors in reasoning or logic, using their silence as a chance to prepare their next response. That might make you an excellent debater, but it doesn't make you a good listener. Good listeners may challenge assumptions and disagree, but the person being listened to feels the listener is trying to help, not wanting to win an argument.

- **Good listeners tend to make suggestions.** Good listening invariably includes some feedback provided in ways that others will accept and that open up alternative paths to consider.

Don't Be a Sponge, Be a Trampoline

This was my favorite part of the *HBR* article "What Great Listeners Actually Do": "While many of us have thought of being a good listener being like a sponge that accurately absorbs what the other person is saying, instead, what these findings show is that good listeners are like trampolines."[26] You can bounce ideas off a truly good listener. In return, rather than merely taking your energy, they deliver energy and clarification back to your own thought process. They are active supporters, increasing your vertical movement and energy level for a metaphorical trampoline effect. It is a fantastic example of brilliance in the basics, because what could be more foundational to success than your employees feeling they've truly been heard?

Great Leaders Speak Last

Have you ever been in a meeting where as soon as the most senior leader in the room starts to share what they think, the brainstorming and volleying of ideas cease? The conversation becomes completely reoriented around the leader's thoughts.

Most leaders, including me, feel like it is our job to state the challenge or opportunity and offer some solutions, then ask what the rest of the team thinks. However, this leads to a phenomenon called "groupthink," which is the practice of thinking or making decisions as a group in a way that discourages creativity or individual responsibility. This is why great leaders speak last.

A true leader in a group is rarely the person who talks the most. It is the person who listens the best. Listening is more than hearing what is said. It is noticing what isn't said. Inviting dissenting views and amplifying quiet voices are further acts of leadership.

> **"There is a difference between listening and waiting for your turn to speak."**
> **—Simon Sinek**

When it comes to meetings, leadership expert and author Simon Sinek has great advice for leaders: "I would say that you need to learn to be the last to speak. The skill to hold your opinions till everyone else has spoken does two things: One, it gives everyone else the feeling they have been heard. It makes everyone else feel that they have contributed. And two, you get the benefit of hearing what everyone else has to think before you render your opinion."[27]

When you wait to hear what your team is going to say, you're giving your team a chance to grow into leaders who can feel comfortable sharing their opinions with each other. It builds team morale and builds more productive discussions because studies have proven that the best teams choose conflict over cohesion and debate each other.[28]

In her article "Why Great Leaders Speak Last," Luba Koziy shares a great tip on how leaders can engage collaboration from their teams in meetings: "First, don't drop an anchor. A group tends to latch onto the first thing said in a meeting. That's one reason the outspoken individual's comment was so persuasive—it created an anchor that the rest of the conversation circled around." She notes that the validity of this verbal anchor isn't as important as it being "dropped" first. "What follows an anchor is a series of adjustments: Each subsequent comment inevitably relates to the anchor comment, until everyone reaches a compromised solution. This is also known as the 'anchoring and adjustment' mental heuristic."[29]

Listen Like You Are Wrong

So how do we have constructive conversations without fear of them turning ugly? We need to train ourselves not to defend our ideas, but rather, explore new ones. One of the best things we have ever heard, but one of the hardest to do, is to "listen as if you are wrong," whether talking to an irate customer, significant other, or anyone who has a different opinion than yours. John admits he might be the only person who argues with someone who agrees with him. He gets more worried when everyone in the conversation appears to all have the same opinions. That is when he tries to play devil's advocate to ensure we are not being narrow-minded or falling prey to groupthink.

Making this approach an integral part of your leadership style is vital. When your leaders learn and practice this style of higher-level communication, it will naturally lead to a superior employee experience.

Chick-fil-A Is America's Favorite Restaurant . . . Again

When CEOs find out that we have consulted with Chick-fil-A, the first question they always ask is, "How do they get 19-year-old kids to be so amazing at customer service?"

At the time of this writing, Chick-fil-A has been ranked America's number one favorite restaurant 10 years in a row by consumers, according to the American Customer Satisfaction Index (ACSI). Even though customers said they prefer full-service restaurants over fast food, that didn't stop customer service leader Chick-fil-A from receiving the highest overall score in the ACSI restaurant survey (which included full service and fast food).[30]

The Customer Experience Is Powered by the Employee Experience
Among national chains, we can look to Chick-fil-A's business model to see why it's an industry leader in the restaurant business, year after year. It goes beyond basics such as food quality, restaurant cleanliness, and speed of service. It's about far more than chicken sandwiches. Chick-fil-A knows there is a direct correlation between customer satisfaction and its employee satisfaction. The process of training employees on delivering superior customer service begins with higher standards in employee selection. This means choosing people with high character and those who exhibit chemistry with existing employees, investing in their training, offering leadership positions, and even supporting their goals outside of their roles at Chick-fil-A. This approach attracts and retains great talent, leads to overall frictionless customer experience, inspires customer loyalty, and keeps the company in the top spot as leader in customer satisfaction.

Why Chick-fil-A Is One of the Most Loved Brands
You know you have a good business problem on your hands when, due to huge demand for your services, the cities in which you operate are trying to declare a public nuisance because of traffic backups, due to the expectations of a stellar customer service experience! Such is the case for multiple cities in which Chick-fil-A operates.

After all these years, Chick-fil-A restaurants are getting better and Chick-fil-A is becoming a brand more and more customers truly can't live without, one for which many a new guest becomes a customer for life.

How does the company create these consumer perceptions and emotional connections? Why does such a high percentage of consumers not only choose but love this brand? It definitely has had its share of obstacles over the past two decades—from explosive

Chicken Sandwiches Are Big Business: Chick-fil-A Just Keeps On Growing

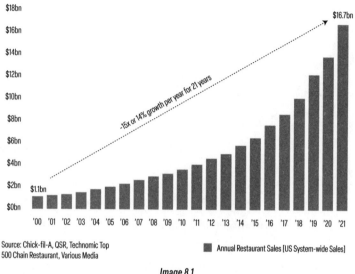

$18bn

$16bn

$14bn

$12bn

$10bn

$8bn

$6bn

$4bn

$2bn $1.1bn

$0bn

~15x or 14% growth per year for 21 years

$16.7bn

'00 '01 '02 '03 '04 '05 '06 '07 '08 '09 '10 '11 '12 '13 '14 '15 '16 '17 '18 '19 '20 '21

Source: Chick-fil-A, QSR, Technomic Top
500 Chain Restaurant, Various Media

■ Annual Restaurant Sales [US System-wide Sales]

Image 8.1

growth, which is usually a customer experience killer, to the Great Recession, the pandemic, and the founders' controversial opinion on same-sex marriages. Regardless of all of this, the one thing that can't be ignored is the incredible success and positive sentiment the brand continues to enjoy, and what other organizations can learn from it.

The average Chick-fil-A freestanding restaurant (non-mall unit) generates more than $8 million in sales a year, which is 54 percent growth over the past five years. With only 2,700 locations, Chick-fil-A generates more total sales than any chain outside of McDonald's and Starbucks. However, Chick-fil-A makes more per restaurant than McDonald's, Subway, and Starbucks combined, even while being closed on Sunday. With such amazing statistics generated by its loyal customers, to merely call it a successful brand would be a huge understatement.

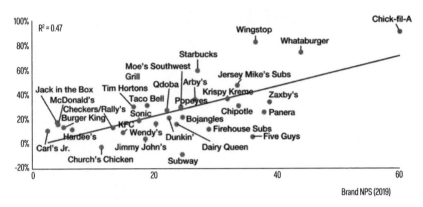

Image 8.2

You can see in Image 8.2 the correlation between Chick-fil-A's best in class net promoter score and best in class same-store overall sales growth.[31]

Even as the demand for Chick-fil-A is at an all-time high, this private restaurant will only grow at a pace that ensures it won't jeopardize the brand experience. This is one of the keys to its success and its distinct brand personality. It could grow ten times faster. However, Chick-fil-A's rigorous selection process for their owner/operators, as well as their obsession with their operational excellence, customer experience, and employee culture will not allow them to compromise any of those factors for more units and higher sales.

Chick-fil-A is meticulous about whom they select to run their restaurants (operators and team leaders) and work in their restaurants (team members). Chick-fil-A's selection process for their operators (aka franchisees) is one of the most impressive by any comparison. The company receives about 20,000 applications a year for franchises and only awards about a hundred new stores annually. How many institutions do you know with a 0.5 percent acceptance rate? For comparison, Harvard University's acceptance rate hovers around 5 percent—about ten times higher than Chick-fil-A's. Even Bain & Company's acceptance rate for 60,000 or so recent college grads who applied for a job last year ran just under 2 percent, reinforcing just how picky Chick-fil-A is in selecting its store operators.[32]

Do Not Go Out Looking for Great Talent; Become a Great Talent Magnet

One of Chick-fil-A's keys to building a world-class brand is that they don't go out and find great talent; great talent finds them. Quality attracts quality, and quality has community impact. Chick-fil-A's widespread reputation for offering a world-class customer experience all but ensures that potential candidates who are only looking for paychecks, those who neither want to be held to a higher standard nor are concerned about making a positive impact, are filtered out.

Chick-fil-A places tremendous importance on selecting amazing leaders. One of their primary decision filters for making informed decisions when selecting the best leaders is asking the following: "Is this someone who cares about others and will pour genuine love and care into their team? And is this someone I would want my child to work for?" Also, is it apparent that these values are part of this potential employee's lifestyle, outside of the workplace?

When the core team of leaders (operators and their top directors) consists of these kinds of people, great talent gets interested. So many companies view recruiting and talent as if it's just "throw out the line and drag in the fish"; however, better yet, what if that fish wants to jump into the boat? Magnets attract, and when you start with a quality core of leaders, quality is reeled in.

Culture Reflects Leadership

On a scale of 1 to 10, what would you rank the culture of the team/department you lead? Is it fantastic (9 or 10)? Or does it have a lot of room for improvement (6 or 7)? Whatever score you give your culture, understand you have just figured out your own rating as a leader.

Do you like your organization's/department's culture? Are you proud of it, or is it lacking? Do you wish you could change many of your employees' attitudes? If you don't like your culture, look in the mirror, because every time, in every organization, culture reflects leadership. How good your organization's or department's culture is, is a direct result of how good you are as a leader. Great leaders create great cultures. You don't even need to take a survey, do studies, or see turnover reports; a culture is something you feel when you walk into a work environment. There is either a strong energy/vibe where everyone understands the organization's purpose and their role in achieving that vision, or something akin to a "fog," a thickness in the air, a place where people are trading hours for dollars.

Grading Your Teams = Grading Your Leaders

One of the best business practices is to create a scoring system for each department/location in your business that considers several key drivers of your team's performance. For example, at the first business John started, John Robert's Spa, for each location, we track the following:

- Sales growth
- Employee engagement scores (morale surveys)
- Employee turnover
- Client retention

We then rank each location by their cumulative grade. Our salon coordinators are incentivized by their quarterly and annual "salon grade." This helps them focus on what is most important, and they are naturally inspired by the competitive nature of where they rank. Like the Navy SEALs example earlier in the chapter, we rotate our salon coordinators to different salon locations, and we have found that a correlation of the team's performance is tied to who their leader is. Think about how unfair it is to your employees on the underperforming team who have been stuck with the same leader for a long time.

This doesn't always mean the leader who has underperforming teams is bad. Many times they were thrown into the position with a lack of leadership training and preparation.

The Importance of Leading People versus Managing the Work They Do

A major part of leadership that is often missed is simply supporting team members. As a matter of fact, Horst Schulze, cofounder of The Ritz-Carlton, was quoted as saying, "A leader should spend 80 percent of their time on their teams."[33] This quote and its percentage make so much sense when you think about it, but it is not always reality in the corporate world.

What Schulze said reiterates the importance of middle managers in today's fast-paced work environments. Managers need to do so much more than simply manage a process or team; they are mentors, guides, and even champions of their team's success.

Let's reflect some more on Schulze's quote, that a leader should spend 80 percent of their time on their teams. Now go back and look at your organization. Is your percentage anywhere close to 80 percent? Chances are good the answer is no.

We once consulted with a sales organization where the leaders had a lot on their plates. Not only were leaders responsible for sales teams of ten to 15 people new to sales, but they were required to maintain their own customer base—they had their own personal sales goals to hit. Because of the demands on time, one leader in the organization actually set up office hours in order to keep his calendar blocked for his own work. The office hours were set up from ten a.m. to eleven a.m. each day—and that was it. That was this managers' only availability to his team—one hour a day, or five hours a week. This organization averaged ten-hour days, so this leader was spending approximately 10 percent of his time supporting his team, and the other 90 percent on other tasks.

The story above is common. When you think about leadership in organizations today, most promotions into management happen because before the promotion, the person was a great employee. The organization wants to reward them, or make sure they do not lose them, so they get the promotion. This happens without any consideration regarding the person's leadership skills and knowledge. Most organizations expect leaders to have leadership skills already within them or that they will pick them up on the job. They don't give this training.

The concept of supporting your team is typically lacking in leadership today. Often too focused on production, revenue, and hitting metrics, today's managers are spending time on tasks as opposed to their teams.

It is incumbent upon organizations to ensure that managers' support of their teams is part of organizational culture, making sure that managers are given the tools to provide support (time being one of the biggest needs) and the training to be successful. If leadership support is not part of your current culture, here are some areas to start:

- Provide Clear Communication

Managers who prioritize transparent and open communication channels establish trust with their team members. Regular updates, clear expectations, and active listening create an environment where ideas and concerns can be freely shared. Organizations need to make sure they are fostering an environment where information is readily available and transparency is the norm.

- Align Goals

Great managers understand the importance of setting clear goals and aligning them with the broader organizational objectives. They work closely with their teams to ensure that individual and team goals are well defined and contribute to the overall mission. When team members see how their efforts tie into the bigger picture, they feel a stronger sense of purpose and motivation. It is also vitally important that managers understand their teams' personal career goals and are looking to coach and mentor along the way.

- Develop Skills

Supportive managers actively identify the strengths and areas of improvement for each team member. They provide opportunities for skill development through training, workshops, and mentorship. This not only enhances individual capabilities but also strengthens the overall team's skill set, leading to a more versatile and adaptable workforce.

- Empower

Micromanagement stifles creativity and hampers growth. Managers who support their teams empower them with the autonomy to make decisions within their areas of responsibility. This empowerment fosters a sense of ownership and can also boost confidence and motivation.

- Recognize

Effective managers never underestimate the power of positive reinforcement. They regularly acknowledge their team's achievements and efforts, whether through public praise or private commendation. Furthermore, constructive feedback is provided in a respectful manner, focusing on growth rather than criticism. This approach helps team members understand their strengths and areas for improvement, thus fostering a continuous learning culture.

- Strive for Work-Life Balance

A manager's support extends beyond the confines of the office. They recognize the importance of work-life balance and encourage their team members to maintain that healthy balance. This also includes an opportunity for the leader to build a relationship with team members, focusing on FORD (family, occupation, recreation, dreams). Knowing this information allows managers to have a better understanding of a team member's work-life balance needs.

- Resolve Conflicts

Conflicts are inevitable in any workplace, but effective managers approach them as opportunities for growth. Rather than avoiding conflicts, they address them promptly and professionally.

- Lead by Example

Managers who embody the values and behaviors they expect from their team members lead by example. They demonstrate a strong work ethic, commitment, and professionalism. This consistency serves as a source of inspiration, motivating team members to follow suit.

9

LEAVING A LEADERSHIP LEGACY

"Your vision needs to be your wildest dream of the impact your organization can have on the world."

Great leaders are paranoid that there is a better way to do something than the way it is currently being done. Great leaders are great visionaries. They never accept the status quo. They are contrarians by nature. They question everything and do not let consensus thinking sway the way they think. They are constantly trying to reimagine a better way.

> **con-trar-i-an (n):**
> Opposing or rejecting popular opinion . . .
> especially a position against the majority

Motivating the Motivators

Emerging leaders need to be taught what success looks like. It starts with having great leaders modeling the behavior. Demonstrating success is inspiring others to achieve more than they thought possible, serving them so they can and celebrating them when they do. Leadership is about making other people better because of your influence.

"Your leadership's emotional commitment is what solves problems that are unsolvable, creates energy when all of the energy has been expended, and ignites emotional commitment in others, including your employee culture," growth guru Stan Slap shares.[1]

Creating Vuja De Moments

A key to helping your mind constantly tinker and reimagine what could be versus what is, is having "vuja de" moments. Vuja de is the opposite of déjà vu. Vuja de is seeing something familiar over and over again, through constant tinkering, experimenting, going down rabbit holes, until it just clicks—an evolution that turns into a revolution. The best way to create a vuja de is through collaboration and constant consuming of information.

As Stan Slap puts it, "There are no new ideas; there are only new combinations of existing ideas."[2] Vuja de can be seen as an intentional mindset or perspective shift, where a person intentionally tries to approach a situation they are familiar with from a new and fresh angle. This can help them to see things in a different light, gain new insights, and approach problems in new ways. It can be a useful tool for creative thinking and problem-solving, as well as for breaking out of ruts and old habits.

What are you consuming?

John asks this question every week to the leaders of his companies. What are you consuming in your area of expertise to make you smarter today than you were yesterday, to ensure you are the smartest person who does what you do?

Now more than ever we need to invest in ourselves and our future. What books and articles are you reading? What podcasts are you listening to? What videos are you watching? What webinars are you attending? This is the number one way you are going to innovate, to reimagine yourself and your business. You should be spending time every day consuming valuable inspiring information.

> "You do not merely want to be considered just the best of the best. You want to be considered the only one who does what you do."

The highest ROI is an investment in knowledge, and no one can ever take it away from you. The most innovative leaders carve out time every day for professional development. There are more opportunities than most people realize. We consume new valuable content daily through audio podcasts, audio books, as well as YouTube and TikTok videos, besides reading blogs and articles. For audio content, we take advantage of listening during workouts, drive times, on airplanes, and even grocery shopping. You wouldn't believe how many hours that adds up to per week.

Consuming content regularly, sharing it with your peers, and then collaborating over each person's takeaways is where the vuja de happens. Often it is information you have heard before but either failed to implement or now see from a new perspective.

Leading in a Crisis

Every company, leader, and human being will face multiple crises in their life, whether it's a recession, pandemic, or a challenging circumstance related specifically to your industry or company. How a leader leads during a crisis will be their narrative and how they're remembered. In times of adversity and change, we discover who we are and what we're made of.

You can't pick and choose when you want to lead. We didn't choose to become a leader because it was always going to be easy. We wanted to be that person others could count on, to take control, who could handle and navigate through any situation no matter its size. When a crisis occurs, that is the time to step up. Your employees are counting on you. They believe in you.

> **"Leadership is easy when the wind is at our back, but much harder when we are facing into the headwinds."**

It is imperative to confidently show all our employees that this crisis is temporary and *will* pass. We need to appreciate the anxiety and stress every employee, fellow leader, vendor, and customer may be having during difficult times. Morale is bound to be low, and we need to do our best to reduce any fear and anxiety.

Crisis Defines Leadership

I, John, personally have found that I am at my best when my companies and I are being challenged or fighting for survival. In a strange way, I am actually comfortable with and become more energized by the obstacles we are facing. That is my nature. While the others are panicking and making short-sighted decisions, my confidence level increases.

I act like I have been waiting for this day; I knew it was coming and I am poised and ready for it. I want everyone in our company to feel they are in the best place they could be. This will be our finest moment.

> **"Tough times don't build character; they reveal it."**

Communicate Like Never Before

During tough times, your employees need to hear more from you than ever before. Not just through emails and texting. Call them, have biweekly Zoom calls. We love what Verne Harnish, growth guru and author, says about leading in a crisis: "I strongly suggest your #1 KPI should be how many minutes of talk time (not texting) you get with colleagues, advisors, friends, and extended family each day—dramatically up your talk time."[3]

Months after the tough times, not one employee will complain by saying, "My boss was so annoying." In all our communication, we need to be 100 percent transparent, especially with our team. Make sure your employees know the sacrifices everyone is making, including the company—for example, tapping into lines of credit, cutting executives' salaries, and so on. Even though sometimes we don't know when or how soon "normal" will return, let them know your short- and long-term strategies. Be in the certainty business.

Tough Times: Tougher Teams

Rough moments will occur in our careers, and often too many people give up. Unless you've got a lot of passion for being a leader, you're not going to survive. Stan Slap wrote a fantastic white paper titled *Tough Times: Tougher Teams*, a fantastic resource when you find yourself leading in a crisis. "Who cares why things suck? What's important is what you do about it; it is the job of management to bring good answers to bad circumstances. 'Whining' is not a strategy. 'Victim' is not a job description. 'Everyone else is in trouble, too' is not management information. Now, let's fix this," Slap shares. "We're at our best when things are at their worst."[4]

Refer to Your Mission, Purpose, Core Values, and Customer Experience Action Statements

Your mission, purpose, core values, and customer experience action statements are the foundation of what your business was built on. Pull them out, talk about what they mean during challenging times. Walk the talk, and constantly be sharing examples of how your people are modeling them through times like this. Great leaders have the ability to communicate with a purpose, rallying and building a community around a clear vision.

A fantastic example of making sure your core values are top of mind for every employee is from Roma Moulding as described in the book *Never Lose an Employee Again*. Headquartered in Ontario, Canada, Roma distributes handcrafted Italian frames to museums, gallery owners, and framers around the world. With a team of 125 employees worldwide, the company focuses on ten core values to drive daily behaviors and a long-term vision.

"To keep these values front and center, while reinforcing

the commitment to these principles across the entire organization, Roma Moulding created core value cards," author Joey Coleman explains. "These colorful cards showcase an image depicting the core value on the front." The back of the card features a blank space for the name of the recipient, followed by a printed message reading, "You Have Exemplified This Core Value in a Way Which Moved, Inspired, & WOW'ed Me! Keep Up the Awesome Work!" Several blank lines allow for a personalized message detailing how the recipient lived the core value, followed by a space for the sender to share their name and the date they awarded the card.

Roma Moulding has core value card stations sprinkled throughout the company. Hanging on walls, positioned next to cubicles, and placed in manufacturing rooms worldwide, the opportunity to grab a card and customize it for a coworker is never more than a few feet away. "Our business is built on caring. When we care about someone they feel an emotion. That emotion creates stickiness. One way to build stickiness within your company is by intentionally showing gratitude," explains CEO Tony Gareri. "If you feel a level of belonging, if you feel that your work is being noticed, if you feel that you love who you work with, that stickiness makes people stay at the company. All we ever want as humans is to belong, and the core value cards help people feel like they belong."[5]

This Isn't Happening TO Us; It Is Happening FOR Us

Find the gift in the crisis. When the pandemic originally hit, The DiJulius Group's leadership team met to discuss how to address ways we were going to handle this pause in our business. We realized, during our brainstorming, that many great initiatives and ideas had come up in the past that we never had the time to properly develop.

These ideas and innovations are critical to our evolution and growth of our brand—new revenue streams, better processes, education, training, and products. Some of these ideas we should have done years ago, and not having done them has hurt the potential growth of our business. This got our entire team excited how we could use this time in such a positive and productive way so when we returned to business as usual, we would be in so much better shape. To the point, the years following the pandemic were our best years ever. We don't think they would have been possible if that crisis had not taken place.

> **"Pressure is a privilege, and it only comes to those who earn it."**
> **—Billie Jean King, US tennis player**

If you're going through tough times, imagine you wake up tomorrow morning and the date is twelve months from today. In vivid detail, what does your world look like? Visualize the best-case scenario for you personally and professionally. While most people don't realize it yet, right now, at this moment, each of us is determining what our next ten years will look like. How will we be defined by a crisis; did we shrink or rise up to conquer it?

How to Reduce the Number One Cause of Anxiety

For most people, uncertainty triggers high extremes of anxiety. As human beings, we like predictability in our lives. That is why so many people are resistant to change. Most of us know, almost within 90 seconds, how long it will take to drive to work or the airport today if we take the same route we take every day. We like sameness, even when it is boring or not meeting our needs. People do the same workouts, go to the same restaurant, even stay in bad relationships because at least they know what they will get versus the unknown, the uncertainty.

Today is all about uncertainty in a world wracked by economic instability, a political divide, and racial unrest. Uncertainty causes anxiety. People would rather know bad news than worry about what could happen. In fact, a study showed that people preferred the option of getting an electric shock now versus the possibility of it happening later.[6]

Uncertainty causes paralysis. Uncertainty causes people to be on edge, react irrationally, and struggle emotionally. Those people are our employees, customers, family members, and even ourselves. If someone struggles with highs and lows, depression, and anxiety issues, times of uncertainty could have a major effect on them. As leaders of businesses, it is our responsibility to try to help reduce our employees' anxiety.

Provide Certainty in All Situations

For starters, you can still provide predictability. How is this possible when we are all dealing with uncertainty and with a lot of things we don't even know the answers to ourselves? Former FBI hostage negotiator Chris Voss says, "Make your world more predictable in tiny little ways. The people you're communicating with don't always know when you're going to have good news, but they shouldn't wonder when you are going to communicate with them. When you don't communicate, the people you lead will be left in uncertainty. Don't let people wonder when you're going to communicate with them. Be fearless about having nothing to say."[7]

Two Leadership Philosophies

John has two leadership philosophies he tries to pass down to his leadership teams and wants all his employees to be aware of:

1. "I will be disappointed if you are going through hard times and do not let us know."

2. "I will be disappointed if you ever miss an important family event."

All About Energy

Energy attracts people like nothing else. People love energy. Energy is about a vibe, a person's spirit, and the fire they have inside of them. Motivational speaker Mel Robbins says it best: "Your energy introduces you before you even speak."

Think about the favorite places you like to hang out. Do you want to walk into a restaurant, bar, or salon with barely anyone inside and employees standing around bored? No way! When that happens, people sometimes say there is a "lack of atmosphere." What's really missing is energy. We love energy—the hustle and bustle of positive movement. When you walk into an Apple Store, you can feel the energy everywhere. People are interacting, playing with products, learning, being educated. This also applies to individuals. We need to focus on the energy we are bringing into a room and into every interaction.

> "It is about how you show up every day; what kind of energy do you bring to others?"

Energy Givers versus Energy Suckers

Science has proven that energy is exchanged between people every time we come into contact with each other.[8] We literally give and receive energy. That can happen in two ways. You can be an "energy giver" bringing positivity and leaving people feeling better for having interacted with you, or your negativity drains them, and you are known as an "energy sucker," also called an energy vampire.

The greatest leaders are the best energy givers consistently. Their presence can change a room. After conversations with these types of leaders, employees get excited about themselves and the critical part they play in the company's success. Leaders with energy make those around them better.

Ask yourself if you are an energy giver or an energy sucker. Just because you high-fived someone this week doesn't make you a full-time energy giver. You have to do it consistently. It has to be a conscious decision, an intentional choice.

ENERGY GIVERS:

- Raise the confidence of everyone they come in contact with
- Improve morale, chemistry, and performance
- Constantly show gratitude and thanks
- Give everyone else the credit
- Believe in others
- Are there for others when they struggle, fail, or are going through hard times
- Are their employees' biggest cheerleaders
- Constantly find out what their employees' goals are and help them achieve those goals

- Are great listeners
- Always build strong relationships and build emotional capital with those around them
- Will walk through fire for those on their team
- Always find a way to give more than their employee was expecting

It is just as important to reflect on the type of people around you. Are you surrounding yourself with energy givers or energy vampires? How do they compare to the list above? Are you hiring and promoting energy givers? Remember, we are the average of the five people we spend the most time with.

> "Don't adapt to the energy in the room; influence the energy in the room."

Encourage = To Put Courage In

Over the past several years, the word "encourage" has become one of John's favorite leadership mantras. The word encourage comes from the old French word *encoragier*, meaning "make strong." Have you ever actually thought about the word "encourage" before? En-Courage = In-Courage. To encourage is to instill courage in another person. When you encourage, you are filling another up with courage.

> "The best thing to do behind someone's back is to pat it."

Finding great people is harder than making good people great. If you want your people to improve, let them overhear the nice things you say about them to others. Are you the leader that, when people talk about their success, will talk about the belief you had in them long before anyone else? Your faith and constant encouragement wouldn't allow them to fail. Want to be successful? Make others successful.

No One Rises to Low Expectations

A study many years ago showed something remarkable about teacher beliefs. Researchers told teachers that some classes of students—across six grade levels—had been tested and were capable of greater intellectual growth than other students. In reality, those students were of the same achievement levels as other students and were randomly chosen for the classes. At the end of one year, the students' scores on IQ tests matched the teachers' false beliefs. When teachers were told that students had higher intellectual ability their students scored at significantly higher levels on IQ tests than students whose teachers were not told anything. This study is a powerful illustration that teachers' expectations and beliefs about students matter.[9]

> "See a man for what he is and he only gets worse, look at him as if he were what he could be and then he becomes what he should be."
> —Goethe

What Gets Recognized Gets Repeated

John was a horrible student when he was growing up. "I was diagnosed with attention deficit disorder, and it was recommended that I repeat every grade in elementary school. For whatever reason, my mother wouldn't allow it. Still, I was a handful for my teachers to deal with," John states.

"When I was in fourth grade, my mother attended a parent-teacher conference, and when she came home, she lectured me about what my teachers had said. When she was finally done listing everything the teachers complained about, I asked, 'Did they say anything nice about me?' My mother paused and said, 'They said you always look nice.' Looking back now, I know that wasn't true. I was a sloppy kid. I had long, messy hair, my clothes were ragtag hand-me-downs, and I am pretty sure I only showered once a week," John continues.

John concludes, "I am positive my mother made up the compliment, but it had a tremendous impact on me. The next morning getting ready for school, I took longer getting dressed and doing my hair because I felt I had a reputation for 'looking nice' that I had to live up to. I can't imagine what might have happened if I'd been told, 'John shows amazing potential in math.'"

> "Never forget, as leaders we are in the human development business."

Vulnerability Is a Strong Leadership Trait

In an interview with the *New York Times*, Walt Bettinger, CEO of Charles Schwab, says early on he assumed his employees only cared about themselves and didn't want to hear about him. "But one of the lessons I learned is that, in the transition from management to leadership, I had to open up. I had to be vulnerable. I had to share with people. In fact, it was more important than anything to share with people the great failures in my life as opposed to the successes," says Bettinger.

"Leadership is something completely different. With leadership, you make a decision every day about whether you choose to follow someone. And you make it in your heart, not your head. The ability to inspire followership is so different than management, and it requires transparency, authenticity, vulnerability and all things that are completely unnatural to you when you are trying to build and achieve and accomplish," explains Bettinger.[10]

Live an extraordinary life so countless others will as a result.

> "Who are you not to be great? Who are you to be ordinary? Who are you to deny greatness? If you would deny it to yourself, you would deny it to the entire world. How dare you to be ordinary?"

As leaders, each of us has the ability to impact thousands of people's lives through providing genuine care and guidance to allow others to reach their fullest potential. It is critical that each of us understand the reason why we were given this amazing gift and honor bestowed on us to lead people. It starts with leading ourselves first.

Our goal shouldn't be to live an extraordinary life so we have a bigger bank account, nicer car, house, and more toys. We need to realize if we live an extraordinary life, so many others will as a result. And if we do not find a way to live an extraordinary life, we end up cheating thousands of people.

Living an extraordinary life is living *fully*. We believe that we all have enormous potential in each of us, and if there are parts of that potential that we do not develop, we are cheating the rest of the world out of the contribution that we could have made. So, if we don't live fully, we don't just deny ourselves a lot of joy and satisfaction; we deny the rest of the people in the world the benefit of what we could have contributed.

Success is when you are firing on all eight cylinders: mentally, physically, emotionally, with family, socially, in your career, financially, and spiritually—all of those are part of you and they all deserve your very best.

Living an extraordinary life is like when the flight attendant says, "You must put your own oxygen mask on first before helping those around you." When you first hear that, it sounds a bit selfish. However, what use will we be to anyone else if we do not take care of ourselves first?

> "Undeveloped potential cheats those around us, those we touch, influence, and impact, as well as deprives ourselves of joy, satisfaction, and opportunities. Living our life to its fullest potential is not an opportunity; it is our responsibility. It is an obligation to be the best version of ourselves we possibly can be every day. Not just for us and how our life will benefit, but also for all the people depending on us: our spouse, children, friends, employees, coworkers, customers, and our community."

Choosing Greatness

My (John) least favorite saying is "I gave my best." To me, it is an unacceptable crutch; I don't want to hear it. My personal feeling is this: When the goal is to accomplish greatness, go where no one or team has gone before—your best won't be good enough. Your best is what you WERE capable of in the past. You have to figure it out, to try a thousand ways; if need be, try a thousand more, innovate, lose sleep, get around it, find loopholes, research, sweat like you never have sweated before.

Every extraordinary accomplishment, invention, or revolution was not a result of someone giving their best. Somehow that person or group found a way to do what no one else could do; they did the impossible; they did what no one had ever done before.

> "Greatness does not choose you; you choose it.
> Greatness is determined by the choices we make every day,
> every hour. The ones who are extraordinary choose to be."

The Reality Distortion Field

Back when Apple was just a start-up, one of the first things new employees were taught, sometimes the hard way, was that their leader, Steve Jobs, "has a reality distortion field."[11] The reality distortion field enabled Jobs to inspire his team to change the course of computing history with a fraction of the resources of Xerox or IBM. They did the impossible because they didn't realize it was impossible.

The reality distortion field was a combination of Jobs's charismatic style, an indomitable will, and an eagerness to bend any fact to fit the purpose at hand. Even though Apple employees were aware of what Jobs was doing, they would eventually give up and go with it. And end up doing the impossible.

Steve Jobs's "reality distortion field" was a personal refusal to accept limitations that stood in the way of his ideas, to convince himself and anyone on his team that anything was in fact possible. Each of us can create such a field. What we consider "possible" and "impossible" are merely the way we were preprogrammed and consensus thinking about artificial boundaries.

What ideas and thoughts do you need to become unrealistic about?

The Power of Our Belief System

For centuries, humans tried to find a way to break the four-minute mile. Legend has it that men were chased by lions to see if that helped them run faster. Unfortunately, that did not end too well. By the early 1950s, medical experts had determined the human body was simply not capable of eclipsing a four-minute-mile pace. It wasn't just dangerous; it was impossible. The human body had reached its limit.

But on May 6, 1954, Roger Bannister made history and shocked the world when he broke the four-minute barrier. The impossible was made possible. Could this feat ever happen again? Within the next 12 months, 24 more runners broke the four-minute mark.

What happened in those 12 months? Did the human anatomy change? No. The belief system of what people thought was possible changed. This applies to every aspect of our lives. What belief system needs to be changed in your world?

> "Great organizations and leaders help their team live a life of purpose."

It all starts with having a vision of what could be. A true purpose is a vision of how you will make the world a better place. A captivating vision inspires people to become evangelists around a movement. It's not the great idea that works; it's the great passion behind it. Every original idea was met with eye rolling and laughing. That is why most ideas are killed long before they can ever become great. If you have a great idea, put on a bulletproof vest and get after it.

Passion is the emotional fuel that drives your vision. It's what you hold on to when your ideas are challenged and people turn you down, when you are rejected by so-called "experts" and the people closest to you. It's the fuel that keeps you going when there is no outside validation for your dream. First, you need to believe in yourself. Don't waiver. There will be people who don't think like you do, don't have your vision, who cannot comprehend the future you see.

You Are a Revolutionary If and Only If . . .

You are fascinated by the future, restless for change, impatient for progress, and deeply dissatisfied with the status quo. As a revolutionary, you are never satisfied with the present, because in your head you can see a better future, and the friction between what is and what could be burns you, stirs you, propels you forward.

WELCOME TO THE
EMPLOYEE EXPERIENCE REVOLUTION

Great companies help people live extraordinary lives. Their leaders inspire employees to build lives of meaning and purpose.

NOTES

INTRODUCTION

1. Orianna Rosa Royle, "Nearly all bosses are 'accidental' with no formal training—and research shows it's leading 1 in 3 workers to quit," *Fortune*, October 16, 2023, https://fortune.com/europe/2023/10/16/bosses -accidental-formal-training-workers-quit-cmi/.

CHAPTER 1

1. "US Overall Customer Satisfaction," American Consumer Satisfaction Index, accessed October 10, 2023, https://www.theacsi.org/the-acsi -difference/us-overall-customer-satisfaction/.

2. Jim Harter, "Is Quiet Quitting Real?," Gallup.com, updated May 17, 2023, https://www.gallup.com/workplace/398306/quiet-quitting-real.aspx.

3. Mary Meisenzahl and Grace Dean, "From Toilet Paper to Candy Bars, Companies Hide Rising Costs by Shrinking the Size of Everyday Products. Here's What That Looks Like," *Business Insider*, updated August 25, 2022, https://www.businessinsider.com/shrinkflation-grocery-stores-pringles -cereal-candy-bars-chocolate-toilet-paper-cadbury-2021-7#gatorade -redesigned-its-32-ounces-bottle-to-be-more-aerodynamic-and-its-easier -to-grab-a-representative-told-quartz-in-march-the-new-design-holds-28 -ounces-a-14-drop-despite-both-bottles-being-the-same-height-2.

4. Matt Phillips and Roberto A. Ferdman, "A Brief, Illustrated History of Blockbuster, Which Is Closing the Last of Its US Stores," Quartz, November 6, 2013, https://www.businessinsider.com/shrinkflation-grocery -stores-pringles-cereal-candy-bars-chocolate-toilet-paper-cadbury-2021 -7#gatorade-redesigned-its-32-ounces-bottle-to-be-more-aerodynamic-and -its-easier-to-grab-a-representative-told-quartz-in-march-the-new-design -holds-28-ounces-a-14-drop-despite-both-bottles-being-the-same-height-2.

5. Fred Reichheld, Darci Darnell, and Maureen Burns, *Winning on Purpose: The Unbeatable Strategy of Loving Customers* (Cambridge, MA: Harvard Business Review Press, 2021), 181–182.

6. Milton Friedman, "A Friedman Doctrine—The Social Responsibility of Business Is to Increase Its Profits," *The New York Times*, September 13, 1970, https://www.nytimes.com/1970/09/13/archives/a-friedman-doctrine-the-social-responsibility-of-business-is-to.html.

7. "Friedman Doctrine," Wikipedia, accessed October 10, 2023, https://en.wikipedia.org/wiki/Friedman_doctrine#cite_note-mf1970-2.

8. Josh Bivens and Jori Kandra, "CEO Pay Has Skyrocketed 1,460% Since 1978," Economic Policy Institute, October 4, 2022, https://www.epi.org/publication/ceo-pay-in-2021/.

9. Becky Simon, "What Is Stakeholder Theory and How Does It Impact an Organization?," Smartsheet, updated August 4, 2023, https://www.smartsheet.com/what-stakeholder-theory-and-how-does-it-impact-organization.

10. R. Edward Freeman, "Shareholders vs. Stakeholders—Friedman vs. Freeman Debate," YouTube, accessed October 10, 2023, https://www.youtube.com/watch?v=_sNKIEzYM7M.

11. Ken Favaro, "The Great Shareholder-Stakeholder Debate," FEI Daily, March 23, 2021, https://www.financialexecutives.org/FEI-Daily/March-2021/The-Great-Shareholder-Stakeholder-Debate.aspx.

12. Favaro, "The Great Shareholder-Stakeholder Debate."

13. Favaro, "The Great Shareholder-Stakeholder Debate."

14. Reichheld, Darnell, and Burns, *Winning on Purpose*, 68.

15. Claes Fornell, "Remarks by the ACSI Chairman," American Consumer Satisfaction Index, accessed October 10, 2023, https://www.theacsi.org/.

16. Reichheld, Darnell, and Burns, *Winning on Purpose*, 63.

17. Reichheld, Darnell, and Burns, *Winning on Purpose*, 64.

CHAPTER 2

1. Scott Galloway, "Advice to Grads: Be Warriors, Not Wokesters," No Mercy/No Malice (blog), https://www.profgalloway.com/advice-to-grads-be-warriors-not-wokesters/.

2. Daymond John, *Rise and Grind: Outperform, Outwork, and Outhustle Your Way to a More Successful and Rewarding Life* (New York: Crown Currency, 2018).

3. K. Badar, "Millennials Cancel Hustle Culture," *Khaleej Times*, December 3, 2021, https://www.khaleejtimes.com/long-reads/millennials-cancel-hustle -culture?amp=1.

4. Jason Fried and David Heinemeier Hansson, *It Doesn't Have to Be Crazy at Work* (New York: Harper Business, 2018); Erin Griffith, "Why Are Young People Pretending to Love Work?," *The New York Times*, January 26, 2019, https://www.nytimes.com/2019/01/26/business/against-hustle -culture-rise-and-grind-tgim.html.

5. Badar, "Millennials Cancel Hustle Culture."

6. Badar, "Millennials Cancel Hustle Culture."

7. Adriana Diaz, "'I Can Do My Job from My Toilet': Majority of Gen Zers Say They Will Soon Quit Jobs for Greater Flexibility and Fulfillment," *New York Post*, October 10, 2023, https://nypost.com/2022/10/18/gen-z -planning-to-quit-jobs-continue-great-gresignation/.

8. Jeremy Salvucci, "What Is the Great Resignation? Definition, Causes & Impact," The Street, updated January 12, 2023, https://www.thestreet.com/ dictionary/g/great-resignation-big-quit-great-reshuffle.

9. Rakesh Kochhar, Kim Parker, and Ruth Igielnik, "Majority of U.S. Workers Changing Jobs Are Seeing Real Wage Gains," Pew Research Center, July 28, 2022, https://www.pewresearch.org/social-trends/2022/07/28/majority-of-u -s-workers-changing-jobs-are-seeing-real-wage-gains/.

10. Kochhar, Parker, and Igielnik, "Majority of U.S. Workers Changing Jobs."

11. Jim Harter, "Is Quiet Quitting Real?," Gallup.com, updated May 17, 2023, https://gallup.com/workplace/398306/quiet-quitting-real.aspx.

12. Kevin A. Hoff, Q. Chelsea Song, Colin J. M. Wee, Wei Ming Jonathan Phan, and James Rounds, "Interest Fit and Job Satisfaction: A Systematic Review and Meta-Analysis," *Journal of Vocational Behavior* 123 (December 2020), 103503, https://doi.org/10.1016/j.jvb.2020.103503.

13. "Gallup's Employee Engagement Survey: Ask the Right Questions with the Q12 Survey," Gallup.com, accessed October 10, 2023, https://www.gallup .com/q12/; Deanna deBara, "The Importance of Employee Engagement," Officevibe, updated September 27, 2023, https://officevibe.com/blog/ importance-employee-engagement.

14. Kim Parker and Rachel Minkin, "What makes for a fulfilling life?," Pew Research Center, September 14, 2023, https://www.pewresearch.org/social -trends/2023/09/14/what-makes-for-a-fulfilling-life/.

15. Tera Allas and Bill Schaninger, "The Boss Factor: Making the World a Better Place Through Workplace Relationships," McKinsey & Company, September 22, 2020, https://www.mckinsey.com/capabilities/people-and -organizational-performance/our-insights/the-boss-factor-making-the-world -a-better-place-through-workplace-relationships.

16. Mary Abbajay, "What to Do When You Have a Bad Boss," *Harvard Business Review*, September 7, 2018, https://hbr.org/2018/09/what-to-do -when-you-have-a-bad-boss.

17. Allas and Schaninger, "The Boss Factor."

18. Clement Bellet, Jan Emmanuel De Neve, and George Ward, "Does employee happiness have an impact on productivity?," Saïd Business School, WP2019-13 (October 14, 2019), https://dx.doi.org/10.2139/ ssrn.3470734.

19. James K. Harter, Theodore L. Hayes, and Frank L. Schmidt, "Business-Unit-Level Relationship between Employee Satisfaction, Employee Engagement, and Business Outcomes: A Meta-Analysis," *Journal of Applied Psychology* 87, no. 2, (April 2002): pp. 268–79, https://doi .org/10.1037/0021-9010.87.2.268.

20. Tom Peters, *The Excellence Dividend* (New York, Vintage, 2018).

21. Jim Clifton, "The Power of Employee Engagement with Jim Clifton," Gary Hamel.com, accessed October 10, 2023, https://www.garyhamel.com/video/ power-employee-engagement-jim-clifton.

22. Steve Jobs, "You've got to find what you love," Goodreads, accessed October 10, 2023, https://www.goodreads.com/quotes/903982-you-ve-got -to-find-what-you-love-and-that-is.

23. Chuck Runyon, "The Great Resignation Is Leading to The Great Inspiration," LinkedIn, May 18, 2022, https://www.linkedin.com/pulse/ great-resignation-leading-inspiration-chuck-runyon/?trk=public_profile_ article_view.

24. Runyon, "The Great Resignation."

25. Chuck Runyon and David Mortensen, *Love Work* (n.p., Beached Whale Press, 2017).

26. Runyon, "The Great Resignation."

27. Runyon, "The Great Resignation."

28. Runyon, "The Great Resignation."

29. Matt Gonzales, "Gallup: Employee Disengagement Hits 9-Year High," SHRM, January 25, 2023, https://www.shrm.org/resourcesandtools/hr -topics/behavioral-competencies/global-and-cultural-effectiveness/pages/ new-gallup-poll-employee-disengagement-hits-9-year-high.aspx.

30. John R. DiJulius III, *The Customer Service Revolution: Overthrow Conventional Business, Inspire Employees, and Change the World* (Austin, TX: Greenleaf, 2015).

31. DiJulius, *The Customer Service Revolution.*

CHAPTER 3

1. Vince Faust, "Tips to Be Fit: Early Retirement May Lead to Earlier Death," *The Philadelphia Tribune*, September 28, 2021, https://www.phillytrib .com/news/health/tips-to-be-fit-early-retirement-may-lead-to-earlier-death/ article_a160f627-8b31-5af8-a095-611c53434e03.html.

2. "Meaning: Keeping Millennials Fired-up," BridgeWorks, accessed October 10, 2023, https://www.generations.com/insights/meaning-keeping -millennials-fired-up.

3. Kathy Durchiek, "Millennial's Desire to Do Good Defines Workplace Culture," SHRM, July 7, 2014, https://www.shrm.org/resourcesandtools/ hr-topics/behavioral-competencies/global-and-cultural-effectiveness/pages/ millennial-impact.aspx.

4. Julie Jargon, "Coffee Talk: Starbucks Chief on Prices, McDonald's Rivalry," *The Wall Street Journal*, updated March 7, 2011, https://www.wsj.com/ articles/SB10001424052748704076804576180313111969984.

5. John R. DiJulius III, *What's the Secret?: To Providing a World-Class Customer Experience* (New York: Wiley & Sons, 2008), 107.

6. DiJulius, *What's the Secret?*

7. Dan Gingiss, *The Experience Maker: How to Create Remarkable Experiences That Your Customers Can't Wait to Share* (New York: Morgan James, 2021).

8. daywireless, "Motorola Solutions—Moments that Matter," YouTube, accessed October 10, 2023, https://www.youtube.com/ watch?v=mbXkwCSxAlA&t=4s.

9. Gingiss, *The Experience Maker.*

10. Lizette Borreli, "Random Acts of Kindness Raise Dopamine Levels and Boost Your Mood," Medical Daily, April 26, 2016, https://www .medicaldaily.com/random-acts-kindness-sweet-emotion-helping-others -dopamine-levels-383563.

11. David Hamilton, "The 5 Side Effects of Kindness," Dr. David R. Hamilton (blog), May 30, 2011, https://drdavidhamilton.com/the-5-side-effects-of -kindness/.

12. Pete Dulcamara, "Humanity-Centric Innovation: Redefining the Meaning of Billionaire," TED, November 2021, https://www.ted.com/talks/pete_dulcamara_humanity_centric_innovation_redefining_the_meaning_of_billionaire/transcript?language=en.

13. Dulcamara, "Humanity-Centric Innovation."

CHAPTER 4

1. "State of the Global Workplace: 2023 Report," Gallup.com, accessed October 11, 2023, https://www.gallup.com/workplace/349484/state-of-the-global-workplace.aspx#ite-350777.

2. Reed Hastings and Erin Meyer, *No Rules Rules: Netflix and the Culture of Reinvention* (London: Virgin Books, 2020).

3. "Statement of Human Rights Principles," California State University, Sacramento, accessed October 11, 2023, https://www.csus.edu/indiv/m/merlinos/enron.html.

4. "Atlassian's Core Values," Atlassian, accessed October 11, 2023, https://www.atlassian.com/company/values.

5. "Atlassian's Core Values," Atlassian, accessed October 28, 2023, https://www.atlassian.com/company/values.

6. "The Columbo Technique," Changing Minds, accessed October 11, 2023, http://changingminds.org/techniques/questioning/columbo_technique.htm.

7. "Principles and Techniques of Motivational Interviewing," AIPC, January 12, 2015, https://www.aipc.net.au/articles/principles-and-techniques-of-motivational-interviewing/.

8. Mark D. Griffiths, "The Psychology of *Columbo*: A Brief Look at the TV Detective's Lessons for Us All," *Psychology Today*, February 20, 2018, https://www.psychologytoday.com/us/blog/in-excess/201802/the-psychology-columbo.

9. Stephanie Clifford, "Would You Like a Smile with That?," *The New York Times*, August 6, 2011, https://www.nytimes.com/2011/08/07/business/pret-a-manger-with-new-fast-food-ideas-gains-a-foothold-in-united-states.html.

10. John DiJulius III, interview with Jesse Cole, September 23, 2020.

11. DiJulius, interview with Jesse Cole.

12. Adam Grant, *Give and Take: Why Helping Others Drives Our Success* (New York: Penguin, 2014).

13. Gene Marks, "Why Does This CEO Insist on Taking Job Candidates Out for Breakfast?" *Entrepreneur*, October 18, 2019, https://www.entrepreneur.com/living/why-does-this-ceo-insist-on-taking-job-candidates-out-for/340934.

14. John DiJulius III, "Why Chick-fil-A Is One of the Most Loved Brands," The DiJulius Group, May 30, 2022, https://thedijuliusgroup.com/why-chick-fil -a-is-one-of-the-most-loved-brands/.

15. Walter Isaacson, *Steve Jobs*, (New York: Simon and Schuster, 2011), 181.

16. Abby Vesoulis, "'If We Had a Panic Button, We'd Be Hitting It.' Women Are Exiting the Labor Force En Masse—and That's Bad for Everyone," *TIME*, October 17, 2020, https://time.com/5900583/women-workforce -economy-covid/.

17. Stephanie Mehta, "Going from The Great Resignation to 'The Great Retention' and other 2022 Priorities," SHRM, January 14, 2022, https:// www.shrm.org/executive/resources/articles/pages/great-retention-.aspx.

18. John DiJulius III, interview with Franco Greco, August 23, 2023.

CHAPTER 5

1. Ben Wigert and Ryan Pendell, "7 Problems With Your Onboarding Program," Workplace, March 1, 2019, https://www.gallup.com/ workplace/247172/problems-onboarding-program.aspx.

2. Joey Coleman, *Never Lose an Employee Again* (New York: Portfolio, 2023).

3. David Burkus, "How to Make New Employees Feel Welcome," David Burkus.com, October 3, 2022, https://davidburkus.com/2022/10/how-to -make-new-employees-feel-welcome/.

4. Burkus, "How to Make New Employees Feel Welcome."

5. Burkus, "How to Make New Employees Feel Welcome."

6. "Onboarding Guide: 5 Steps for New Employees," Indeed, accessed October 11, 2023, https://www.indeed.com/hire/c/info/onboarding -guide?co=US.

7. Coleman, *Never Lose an Employee Again*, 127.

8. "Verbit's 'Buddy Program' Hoped to Make Onboarding a Little Easier during Covid-19," CTech, accessed October 11, 2023, https://www .calcalistech.com/ctech/articles/0,7340,L-3898996,00.html.

9. Verne Harnish, "Powerful $20 First Impression," LinkedIn, accessed October 11, 2023, https://www.linkedin.com/posts/verneharnish_ verneharnish-scalingup-ceobootcamp-activity-7062426132477857794-Xt -N/?utm_source=share&utm_medium=member_desktop.

10. John DiJulius III, interview with Franco Greco, August 23, 2023.

11. John DiJulius III, interview with Rob Posner, August 23, 2023.

12. DiJulius, interview with Franco Greco.

CHAPTER 6

1. Abigail Johnson Hess, "LinkedIn: 94% of Employees Say They Would Stay at a Company Longer for This Reason—And It's Not a Raise," CNBC, February 27, 2019, https://www.cnbc.com/2019/02/27/94percent-of -employees-would-stay-at-a-company-for-this-one-reason.html.

2. "Building the Agile Future," LinkedIn, accessed October 11, 2023, https:// learning.linkedin.com/resources/workplace-learning-report;

3. Jane Courtnell, "Reduce Employee Turnover by 63% Using Employee Acknowledgment," Process.St, March 29, 2021, https://www.process.st/ employee-acknowledgment/.

4. *Gallup: State of the American Workplace 2017*, https://compass.arizona .edu/sites/compass.arizona.edu/files/Gallup_State_of_the_American_ Workplace_Report_2017%5B1%5D.pdf.

5. Adam Bryant, "Walt Bettinger of Charles Schwab: You've Got to Open Up to Move Up," *The New York Times*, February 4, 2016, https://www .nytimes.com/2016/02/07/business/walt-bettinger-of-charles-schwab-youve -got-to-open-up-to-move-up.html.

6. Jim Harter and Amy Adkins, "Employees Want a Lot More from Their Managers," Gallup.com, April 8, 2015, https://www.gallup.com/ workplace/236570/employees-lot-managers.aspx.

7. Jim Clifton, "The Power of Employee Engagement with Jim Clifton," Gary Hamel.com, accessed October 11, 2023, https://www.garyhamel.com/video/ power-employee-engagement-jim-clifton.

8. John Ruhlin, *Giftology: The Art and Science of Using Gifts to Cut Through the Noise, Increase Referrals, and Strengthen Client Retention* (n.p., Lioncrest Publishing, 2016) 38.

9. *Authority Magazine* Editorial Staff, "'Chief Fun Officer' Rebecca Binnendyk: Five Things Business Leaders Can Do to Create a Fantastic Work Culture," Medium, January 20, 2021, https://medium.com/authority -magazine/chief-fun-officer-rebecca-binnendyk-five-things-business-leaders -can-do-to-create-a-fantastic-24cc3dc5e211.

10. "Mind Share Partners' 2021 Mental Health at Work Report," Mind Share Partners, accessed October 12, 2023, https://www.mindsharepartners.org/ mentalhealthatworkreport-2021.

11. "Stress in America 2022: Concerned for the Future, Beset by Inflation," American Psychological Association, accessed October 31, 2023, https:// www.apa.org/news/press/releases/stress/2022/concerned-future-inflation.

12. Garen Staglin, "It's Time for Employers to Support Youth Mental Health," *Forbes*, May 2, 2022, https://www.forbes.com/sites/onemind/2022/05/02/its-time-for-employers-to-support-youth-mental-health/?sh=37e5ff765ce5.

13. *Fast Company* Staff, "Mental Health at Work: It's (Finally) Time to Talk about It," *Fast Company*, May 2, 2022, https://www.fastcompany.com/90740173/mental-health-at-work-its-finally-time-to-talk-about-it.

14. Kathleen Davis, "This Is What Real Mental Health Support at Work Looks Like," *Fast Company*, December 20, 2021, https://www.fastcompany.com/90706165/this-is-what-real-mental-health-support-at-work-looks-like.

15. Katherine Dillinger, "Surgeon General Lays Out Framework to Tackle Loneliness and 'Mend the Social Fabric of Our Nation,'" CNN Health, May 2, 2023, https://www.cnn.com/2023/05/02/health/murthy-loneliness-isolation/index.html.

16. "Health Risks of Social Isolation and Loneliness," CDC, accessed October 12, 2023, https://www.cdc.gov/emotional-wellbeing/social-connectedness/loneliness.htm.

17. Dillinger, "Surgeon General Lays Out Framework."

18. Robert Kegan, Lisa Laskow Lahey, Matthew L. Miller, Andy Fleming, and Deborah Helsing, *An Everyone Culture: Becoming a Deliberately Developmental Organization* (Cambridge, MA: Harvard Review Press, 2016).

19. "Culture Spotlight: Next Jump, the Company Which Never Fires Anyone for Performance Reasons," Charlie HR, accessed October 28, 2023, https://www.charliehr.com/blog/next-jump-ddo/.

20. "Culture Spotlight: Next Jump."

21. Hayley Peterson, "Why Chick-fil-A's Restaurants Sell 3 Times as Much as KFC's," *Insider*, May 10, 2016, https://www.businessinsider.com/why-chick-fil-a-is-so-successful-2016-5.

22. Peterson, "Why Chick-fil-A's Restaurants Sell."

23. John DiJulius III, interview with Ryan Magnon, summer 2021.

24. DiJulius, interview with Ryan Magnon.

25. *2019 State of One-on-Ones Report*, SoapBox, accessed October 12, 2023, https://hypercontext.com/wp-content/uploads/2019/11/soapbox-state-of-one-on-ones-report.pdf.

26. *2019 State of One-on-Ones Report*.

27. "The Complete Guide to One on One Meetings with Employees," Qualtrics, accessed October 12, 2023, https://www.qualtrics.com/experience-management/employee/one-on-one-meeting/.

28. Ryan Fuller and Nina Shikaloff, "What Great Managers Do Daily," *Harvard Business Review*, December 14, 2016, https://hbr.org/2016/12/what-great-managers-do-daily.

29. Kim Scott, "Why Praising in Public and Criticizing in Private is Key to Giving Feedback Others Will Act On," Radical Candor (blog), accessed October 12, 2023, https://www.radicalcandor.com/blog/public-praise-private-criticism/.

CHAPTER 7

1. Dave Murray, personal conversation with Jay Juffre, August 2023.

2. Dave Murray, personal conversation with Stephanie Kohl, 2017.

3. John R. DiJulius III, *The Relationship Economy: Building Stronger Customer Connections in the Digital Age* (Austin, TX: Greenleaf, 2014), 168.

4. Charlotte-Mecklenburg Police Department, "CMPD Serves: A Day in the Life of a CMPD Employee," YouTube, accessed October 12, 2023, https://www.youtube.com/watch?v=p2VahcyTT4Y.

5. John DiJulius III, "'Shrinkflation': Learning to Recognize and Navigate the Customer Service Recession," The DiJulius Group, September 12, 2022, https://thedijuliusgroup.com/shrinkflation-learning-to-recognize-and-navigate-the-customer-service-recession/.

6. Preetika Rana, "What Happened When Uber's CEO Started Driving for Uber," *The Wall Street Journal*, April 7, 2023, https://www.wsj.com/articles/uber-ceo-started-driving-for-uber-5bef5023; Paige McGlauflin, "The CEOs of Uber and Starbucks Are Picking Up Frontline Shifts. The Trend Is a 'No-Brainer' for Driving Employee Satisfaction," *Fortune*, April 20, 2023, https://fortune.com/2023/04/20/uber-starbucks-ceo-frontline-shifts-employee-satisfaction/?showAdminBar=true.

7. Kim Parker and Juliana Menasce Horowitz, "Majority of Workers Who Quit a Job in 2021 Cite Low Pay, No Opportunities for Advancement, Feeling Disrespected," Pew Research Center, March 9, 2022, https://www.pewresearch.org/short-reads/2022/03/09/majority-of-workers-who-quit-a-job-in-2021-cite-low-pay-no-opportunities-for-advancement-feeling-disrespected/.

8. Christopher Pappas, "The Future of Work Report: Are Company Leaders Out of Touch with What Employees Want?," eLearning Industry, November 22, 2022, https://elearningindustry.com/the-future-of-work-report-are-company-leaders-out-of-touch-with-what-employees-want.

9. Michael E. Porter and Nitin Nohria, "How CEOs Manage Time," *Harvard Business Review*, July–August 2018, https://hbr.org/2018/07/how-ceos -manage-time.

10. Trey Williams, "Airbnb's CEO Spent 6 Months Living in His Company's Rentals—and Found the Core Problem with His Business," *Fortune*, May 4, 2023, https://fortune.com/2023/05/04/airbnb-ceo-brian-chesky-lessons -rentals/?showAdminBar=true.

CHAPTER 8

1. Orianna Rosa Royle, "Nearly All Bosses Are 'Accidental' with No Formal Training—and Research Shows It's Leading 1 in 3 Workers to Quit," *Forbes*, October 16, 2023.

2. Tera Allas and Bill Schaninger, "The Boss Factor: Making the World a Better Place Through Workplace Relationships," McKinsey & Company, September 22, 2020, https://www.mckinsey.com/capabilities/people-and -organizational-performance/our-insights/the-boss-factor-making-the-world -a-better-place-through-workplace-relationships.

3. Reed Hastings and Erin Meyer, *No Rules Rules: Netflix and the Culture of Reinvention* (London: Virgin Books, 2020).

4. Hastings, *No Rules Rules*.

5. Never Give Up, "Jeff Bezos on Failures at Amazon," YouTube, accessed October 12, 2023, https://www.youtube.com/watch?v=I9CKa90Leh0; S. Pangambam, "Jeff Bezos's Life Changing Advice for You (Full Transcript)," *The Singju Post*, December 19, 2018, https://singjupost.com/jeff-bezoss-life -changing-advice-for-you-full-transcript/.

6. "Jeff Bezos on Failures at Amazon"; Pangambam, "Jeff Bezos's Life Changing Advice for You."

7. Jocko Willink and Leif Babin, *Extreme Ownership: How U.S. Navy SEALs Lead and Win* (New York: St. Martin's Press, 2015).

8. Denise Linda Parris and Jon Welty Peachey, "A Systematic Literature Review of Servant Leadership Theory in Organizational Contexts," *Journal of Business Ethics* 111, no. 3 (March 2013): 377–93, https://www.jstor.org/ stable/23433856.

9. Randall Beck and James Harter, "Why Good Managers Are So Rare," *Harvard Business Review*, March 13, 2014, https://hbr.org/2014/03/why -good-managers-are-so-rare.

10. Tomas Chamorro-Premuzic, "Why Do So Many Incompetent Men Become Leaders?," *Harvard Business Review*, August 22, 2013, https://hbr .org/2013/08/why-do-so-many-incompetent-men.

11. Paul J. Zak, "How Stories Change the Brain," *Greater Good*, December 17, 2013, https://greatergood.berkeley.edu/article/item/how_stories_ change_brain.

12. "(Better) Leadership: Resources for Leading With Compassion, Wellbeing & Belonging," Center for Creative Leadership, accessed October 12, 2023, https://www.ccl.org/articles/white-papers/towards-better-leadership -resources-for-compassion-wellbeing-belonging/.

13. Ed Yong, "The Incredible Thing We Do During Conversations," *The Atlantic*, January 4, 2016, https://www.theatlantic.com/science/ archive/2016/01/ the-incredible-thing-we-do-during-conversations/422439/.

14. Brian Greene, Chelsea Catlett, Daryl Chen, Oliver Friedman, Tom Carter, and Yasmin Belkhyr, "Humanizing Our Future: A Night of Talks from TED and Verizon," TEDBlog, September 25, 2018, https://blog.ted.com/ humanizing-our-future-a-night-of-talks-from-ted-and-verizon/.

15. "A Better Way to Measure and Value Business Relationships," The Relational Capital Group, April 2010, https://www.relationalcapitalgroup .com/downloads/EnterpriseRQ-whitepaper.pdf.

16. Fred Reichheld, Darci Darnell, and Maureen Burns, *Winning on Purpose: The Unbeatable Strategy of Loving Customers* (Cambridge, MA: Harvard Business Review Press, 2021), 77.

17. John R. DiJulius III, *The Relationship Economy: Building Stronger Customer Connections in the Digital Age* (Austin, TX: Greenleaf, 2014), 81.

18. Jack Zenger and Joseph Folkman, "What Great Listeners Actually Do," *Harvard Business Review*, July 14, 2015, https://hbr.org/2016/07/what -great-listeners-actually-do.

19. Jason Sudeikis, Bill Lawrence, Brendan Hunt, and Joe Kelly, *Ted Lasso*, season 1, episode 8, "The Diamond Dogs," originally aired September 18, 2020, on Apple TV.

20. Jessica Stillman, "3 Habits That Will Increase Your Empathy," *Inc.*, August 22, 2014, https://www.inc.com/jessica-stillman/3-habits-that-will-increase -your-empathy.html.

21. Scott Gerber and Ryan Paugh, *Superconnector: Stop Networking and Start Building Business Relationships that Matter* (New York: Da Capo Press, 2018).

22. Tom Peters, *The Excellence Dividend: Meeting the Tech Tide with Work That Wows and Jobs That Last* (New York: Vintage Books, 2018).

23. Peters, *The Excellence Dividend*.

24. Rich Simmonds, "The Art of Listening . . . Leading and Selling," Rich Simmonds, May 7, 2015, http://richsimmondsza.com/2015/05/07/ the-art -of-listening-leading-and-selling/.

25. Jack Zenger and Joseph Folkman, "What Great Listeners Actually Do," *Harvard Business Review*, July 14, 2016, https://hbr.org/2016/07/what -great-listeners-actually-do.

26. Zenger and Folkman, "What Great Listeners Actually Do."

27. Simon Sinek, "Be the Last to Speak," Goalcast, accessed October 30, 2023, https://www.goalcast.com/simon-sinek-be-the-last-to-speak/.

28. Monica Torres, "This Is the Secret Behind Top Teams' Best Ideas," Ladders, October 12, 2017, https://www.theladders.com/career-advice/debate-secret -behind-top-teams-best-ideas.

29. Luba Koziy, "Why Great Leaders Speak Last," SmartBrief, January 29, 2021, https://corp.smartbrief.com/authors/luba-koziy; Nicholas Epley and Thomas Gilovich, "The Anchoring-and-Adjustment Heuristic: Why the Adjustments Are Insufficient," *Psychological Science* 17, no. 4 (2006): 311–318, https://doi.org/10.1111/j.1467-9280.2006.01704.x.

30. Alicia Kelso, "Chick-fil-A Ranked No. 1 for Customer Satisfaction for the 9th Straight Year, *Nation's Restaurant News*, June 27, 2023, https://www .nrn.com/consumer-trends/chick-fil-ranked-no-1-customer-satisfaction-9th -straight-year.

31. Reichheld, Darnell, and Burns, *Winning on Purpose*, 131.

32. Reichheld, Darnell, and Burns, *Winning on Purpose,* 131.

33. This quote was shared by Ryan Magnon, VP Quality Capella Hotel Group, 2011.

Chapter 9

1. Stan Slap, "Tough Times: Tougher Teams," SLAP, accessed October 13, 2023, https://slapcompany.com/t4/.

2. Slap, "Tough Times: Tougher Teams."

3. Verne Harnish, "Talk, Talk, Talk And Then Talk Some More," *Chief Executive*, accessed October 30, 2023, https://chiefexecutive.net/talk-talk -talk-and-then-talk-some-more/.

4. Slap, "Tough Times: Tougher Teams."

5. Joey Coleman, *Never Lose an Employee Again* (New York: Portfolio, 2023).

6. Nadia Whitehead, "People Would Rather Be Electrically Shocked Than Left Alone with Their Thoughts," *Science*, July 3 2014, https://www.science.org/content/article/people-would-rather-be-electrically-shocked-left-alone-their-thoughts.

7. Chris Voss, "Session Notes—Facing Fear in Uncertain Situations, Featuring Chris Voss," Global Leadership Network, accessed October 30, 2023, https://globalleadership.org/articles/leading-yourself/session-notes-facing-fear-in-uncertain-situations-featuring-chris-voss/?locale=en.

8. "What Is Spiritual Energy Exchange? 3 Ways It Can Happen," Enhanced, https://enhancedapp.io/what-is-spiritual-energy-exchange/.

9. "When You Believe In Your Students They Do Better," Stanford Education, accessed October 13, 2023, https://www.youcubed.org/evidence/believe-students-better/.

10. Adam Bryant, "Walt Bettinger of Charles Schwab: You've Got to Open Up to Move Up," *The New York Times*, February 4, 2016, https://www.nytimes.com/2016/02/07/business/walt-bettinger-of-charles-schwab-youve-got-to-open-up-to-move-up.html.

11. Rob Beschizza, "How Steve Jobs' Reality Distortion Field Works," *Wired*, January 29, 2000, https://www.wired.com/2008/01/how-steve-jobs/.

ABOUT THE AUTHORS

JOHN DiJULIUS III is known as the authority on helping organizations build a world-class customer and employee experience. He is the best-selling author of six books. John is the founder and chief revolution officer of The DiJulius Group, which has worked with companies such as The Ritz-Carlton, Lexus, Starbucks, KeyBank, Nestlé, Chick-fil-A, Celebrity Cruises, Bristol-Myers, Marriott, and many more, helping them make the experience they deliver their single biggest competitive advantage. John helps companies become the brand customers can't live without and make price irrelevant. John is also the founder of John Robert's Spas, one of the Top 20 Salons in America, and the founder of a nonprofit, Believe in Dreams.

DAVE MURRAY is The DiJulius Group's vice president of consulting. Dave is a master at helping companies create real change that sticks. He excels at communication and easily bridges the gap between corporate leaders and front-line team members. His passion for building ideal environments leads teams toward attaining award-winning customer satisfaction, best-place-to-work achievements, and record-breaking profits. He has over 30 years of experience in customer service. His background in the sports and entertainment industry gives him an uncommon understanding of marketplace competition and high expectations. Unflappable and highly respected, Dave Murray is one of today's leading customer experience strategists.